A LIE TOL

---------- B_____

THE

TRUTH

EXPOSING HOW THE WATCHTOWER DECEIVES

JEHOVAH'S WITNESSES

ERIC SCHAEFFER

Index

PART FOUR

CONCLUSION:

APENDIX

The Most Destructive Weapon

What is the most destructive weapon of all time? Is it a stick? A rock... Sword... Gun... Atomic Bomb? Each of these is responsible for their fair share of pain and suffering, but none have come close to the amount of destruction caused by one other weapon. This weapon does not look like other weapons and it appears far less threatening. Most of the time, its work goes unnoticed by its victims. One minute, it can be seen in a room full of military advisors, and the next it can be in the hands of a man sitting on a park bench. It can be waved overhead by an angry mob, and it can be beside a mother as she feeds her baby.

When an enemy wants to conquer a group of people, his or her first tactic is not always physical harm. Their first and often most successful tactic is to change people's minds. After all, why should an enemy try to kill a group of people when he or she can make them slaves?

Propaganda is the most destructive weapon of all time. The art of deceiving the masses has been responsible for more pain and suffering than anyone can calculate. All a strategic enemy has to do is articulate his or her deception in a convincing way, then repeat it so often that the people begin to embrace it. In other words, "A lie told often enough becomes the truth."

What makes propaganda so powerful is that people don't know they are under attack until it is too late. In this way, it can be compared with rat poison. Rat poison is made up of 95% corn, and 5% poison. When an unsuspecting rodent comes upon it, he thinks it is safe to eat because the majority of rat poison smells like food and tastes like food, but it is the 5% that will kill him. Likewise, the most effective lie is the one wrapped in truth. The New World Translation of the Holy Scriptures, for example, has many chapters and verses that are in line with the Bible's original message, but it is the 5% that will corrupt your soul and separate you from God.

The goal of this book is to provide the reader with undeniable evidence that the Watchtower deceives Jehovah's Witnesses by twisting God's message. This will be accomplished through a comparative study of the New World Translation, other Bibles, the original language, historical evidence, and the Watchtower's own material. Therefore, it is the hope of the author that the reader will take the time to test and approve this material, not with an indoctrinated and biased perspective, but with equal scales and sound scholarship.[1] [2]

[1] Inside and Outside Cover, New World Translation of the Holy Scriptures, Watchtower Bible And Tract Society, New York, Jan 1, 2013

[2] Note: This text will be comparing the New World Translation (NWT) with the English Standard Version (ESV). However, a comparison between the New World Translation and other commonly used Bibles (ASV, KJV, NASB, NIV, NRSV, NLT, AMP, etc.) will produce similar results.

PART ONE

THE TEST OF A TRUE PROPHET IS TIME

In a publication called, *How to Be Worthy of TRUST*, the Watchtower made the following statement,

"JEHOVAH GOD is the Grand Identifier of his true messengers. He identifies them by making the messages he delivers through them come true. Jehovah is also the Great Exposer of false messengers. How does He expose them? He frustrates their signs and predictions. In this way he shows that they are self-appointed prognosticators, whose messages really spring from their own false reasoning – yes, their foolish, fleshly thinking!"[3]

This was published on May 1, 1997, after well over a hundred years of Watchtower teachings, prophecies, and predictions.

With such a bold statement, one would naturally assume the Watchtower has a long history of truth and credibility. After all, Jehovah's Witness have been the grand defenders of Watchtower doctrine throughout their existence. Surely the organization has a track record that surpasses all expectation, a proverbial "solid rock" if you will.

This inspired me to take a little journey through Watchtower publications to see how consistent and faithful they have been over the years.

---

[3] *The Watchtower*, May 1, 1997 page 8

Chapter One

Solid Rock or Shifting Sand?

I started my journey with a 1931 Watchtower publication known as *The Golden Age*. A section of this journal discusses their view of vaccinations:

"Vaccination is a direct violation of the everlasting covenant that God made with Noah after the flood... Of all the inventions that have been foisted upon mankind for their defilement, the most suddenly devilish is that of vaccination."[4]

I was surprised by the Watchtower's stance here. I had no idea Jehovah's Witnesses were so opposed to vaccinations. But then I found some of their other writings on this subject. The Watchtower December 15, 1952 reads,

"The matter of vaccination is one for the individual that has to face it to decide for himself... After consideration of the matter is does not appear to us to be in violation of the everlasting covenant made with Noah."[5]

---

[4] *The Golden Age*, Feb. 4, 1931 p. 293 and 295
[5] *The Watchtower*, Dec. 15, 1952, p. 764

I wonder what caused them to take the opposite stance on vaccination? Considering the amount of trust Jehovah's Witness have in the Watchtower, I assume this must be some kind of fluke. So I decided to investigate another subject.

Birthdays…Jehovah's Witnesses are very passionate about birthdays. Surely the Watchtower has consistency on this subject! The Watchtower January 1, 1940 reads,

"I appreciate the photograph which came to me on the morning after the eighth, which was my 80th birthday. It was indeed a birthday gift from Jehovah to be used in proclaiming his name."[6]

---

[6] *The Watchtower*, Jan. 1, 1940, p. 16

But when I go to JW.org, on their page titled, *Why Don't Jehovah's Witnesses Celebrate Birthdays*, it reads,

> "Jehovah's Witnesses do not celebrate birthdays because they believe such celebrations displease God... Birthday celebrations have pagan roots."[7]

Wow! I wonder, if Jehovah knew birthday celebrations have pagan roots when He sent that man his birthday gift?

Maybe we should look at Christmas! Perhaps we will find better consistency in the area of Christmas! That's another thing Jehovah's Witnesses are extremely passionate about! The Watchtower December 1, 1904 says,

> "We may as well join with a civilized world in celebrating the grand event on the day

---

[7] JW.org, Jehovah's Witnesses, *Why Don't Jehovah's Witnesses Celebrate Birthdays?* https://www.jw.org/en/jehovahs-witnesses/faq/birthdays/

which the majority celebrate – Christmas day."[8]

[9] Pictured is a Christmas morning at Bethel. A number of Jehovah's Witnesses, including Watchtower president, Judge Rutherford, celebrate around presents and mistletoe.

But then the Watchtower says in their page, *Why Don't Jehovah's Witnesses Celebrate Christmas*:

[8] *The Watchtower*, Dec. 1, 1904 p. 364
[9] JWfacts, *Christmas, Birthdays, Mother's Day & Flag Salute*, https://www.jwfacts.com/watchtower/celebrations.php

"We believe that Christmas is not approved by God because he's rooted in pagan customs and rights."[10]

What is going on with all of this back and forth? Was Jehovah speaking for the Organization when he said, "Celebrate Christmas" or was Jehovah speaking when he said, "Don't celebrate Christmas"? This is very confusing. I wonder why Jehovah's Witnesses have such a strong trust in the Watchtower after such inconsistencies?

Let's try one more time to find some consistency in Watchtower doctrine. Jesus worship! What could be more fundamental to one's doctrine than that? Surely the Watchtower is consistent in its stance on Jesus! The Watchtower, 1880 says,

---

[10] JW.org, Jehovah's Witnesses, *Why Don't Jehovah's Witnesses Celebrate Christmas?*
https://www.jw.org/en/jehovahs-witnesses/faq/why-not-celebrate-christmas/

"He was the object of unreproved worship even when a babe, by wise men who came to see the new-born King... Even the angels delighted to do Him honor. 'When He bringeth the first-begotten into the world, He saith, "And let all the angels of God worship Him."[11]

"Jehovah God commands all to worship Christ Jesus because Christ Jesus is the express image of his Father, Jehovah."[12]

[11] *Zion's Watch Tower*, 1880 Oct, page 144
[12] *The Watchtower*, 1939 Nov 15, page 339

"Jehovah God now reigns as King by means of his capital organization Zion, then whosoever would worship Him must also worship and bow down to Jehovah's Chief One in that capital organization, namely, Christ Jesus, his Co-regent on the throne of The Theocracy."[13]

But then something unthinkable happened. After several decades of worshipping Jesus, the Watchtower suddenly decided it was not good for Jehovah's Witnesses to do this any longer! Their January 1, 1954 publication made it official:

---

[13] *The Watchtower*, 1945 Oct 15, page 313

"No distinct worship is to be rendered to Jesus."[14]

All of these subjects are important to Jehovah's Witnesses. Too important, I would say, to be changing their stance. The passion Jehovah's Witnesses express for topics like Christmas or Jesus worship is so strong, one marvels that their religion used to teach the opposite.

This journey through Watchtower doctrine has led me to believe the Watchtower is not very consistent in their teaching. Perhaps they have a better track record in their Armageddon prophecies and predictions?

---

[14] *The Watchtower*, 1954 Jan 1, page 31

Chapter Two

"The Sky is Falling!"

I recently saw a cartoon clip that reminded me of Jehovah's Witness history. There was a little duck walking along the woods when a wolf spotted him. Realizing he was in danger; the duck ran as fast as he could while the wolf chased. The duck narrowly escaped by entering a fortress the wolf could not penetrate. This upset the wolf, so he took a brick, threw it over the wall and just happened to hit the duck in the head.

This surprised the duck. So much so, he thought the sky was falling. So, he went to his friends and said, "The sky is falling! The sky is falling!" His friends laughed at first, but when the wolf hit them on the head too, they believed the duck's story. They all ran in a panic yelling, "The sky is falling! The sky is falling!" This is when the wolf shouted, "Hey, you'd better go to the king!" They believed him, so they all left the safety of the fortress and ran to the king, who happened to be the wolf in disguise.

When they got to the "king," they told him, "The sky is falling! The sky is falling!" So, the "king" said, "Oh yes, let me help you with that. Run in here and you will be safe." And he led them right into a furnace. Once they got in, he slammed the door shut and laughed, "Ha, ha, ha, you fools!"

This reminds me of Jehovah's Witness history because they too have a long history of being told, "The sky is falling!" The Watchtower has told them many times that the world will end and they had better run to the king, they better run to Jehovah to keep them safe. But little do the Jehovah's Witnesses know, this doctrine will lead them right into a furnace they do not want to go.

This started in 1889, when Charles Taze Russell, the founder of the Jehovah's Witnesses, produced a book tilted, *The Time is at Hand*. In it he made predictions for the end of the world.

"In view of the strong Bible evidence concerning the Times of the Gentiles, we consider it an established truth that the final end of the kingdom of this world, and the full establishment of the Kingdom of God, will be accomplished by the end of A.D. 1914."[15]

One year later, the Watchtower magazine backed up Russell's book in its October 1890 publication:

---

[15] *The Time is at Hand*, Tower Publishing Company, Allegheny PA, 1889, page 99

> "The Millennium of peace and blessing would be introduced by forty years of trouble, beginning slightly in 1874 and increasing until social chaos should prevail in 1914…"[16]

In a July 15, 1894 magazine, the Watchtower made it very clear this was not their idea, but the date for the end of the world came directly from Jehovah:

> "We see no reason for changing the figures — nor could we change them if we would. They are, we believe, God's dates, not ours. But bear in mind that the end of 1914 is not the date for the beginning, but for the end of the time of trouble."[17]

As you can imagine, all these predictions brought a high level of anticipation and anxiety. However, 1914 came and went without incident. How can this be? The Watchtower claims to be Jehovah's mouthpiece to the world. Was Jehovah mistaken? Perhaps He changed His mind? Whatever the reason, it forced the Watchtower to push back

---

[16] *The Watchtower*, October 1890, page 1243
[17] *The Watchtower*, July 15, 1894, page 1677

Jehovah's time of Armageddon an additional year to 1915. This too was uneventful, so they pushed Jehovah back three more years to 1918. And again, Jehovah refused to act.

Prior to this 1918 prophecy, Charles Taze Russell died from complications relating to diverticulitis. But the false prophecies did not die with Russell. The organization's second president, Judge Rutherford started predicting the end of the world will take place in 1925. He wrote a book called, *Millions now living will never die.*[18]

---

[18] J. F. Rutherford, *Millions Now Living Will Never Die*, International Bible Students Association, Brooklyn NY, 1920

This book's message boasted that millions of Jehovah's Witnesses will never experience death because the end will take place before they die.

This caused no little stir. Rutherford himself travelled to share Jehovah's message with as many as possible. To back up this material, the Watchtower distributed a bulletin to promote the end of the world. It was a guide to assist Jehovah's Witnesses in introducing this topic to others. It said,

[19]"Good morning!

Do you know that millions now living will never die?

I mean just what I say – that millions now living are never going to die…

[The] work of Pastor Russell, tells why there are millions now living who will never die; and if you can keep alive until 1925 you have excellent chances of being one of them…

It is an absolute fact, stated in every book of the Bible, foretold by every prophet of the Bible. I believe you will agree that this subject is well worth a few evenings' time for investigation."

Friends, this is pure propaganda! When did the Bible ever say 1925 will be the end? When did "all the

<hr>

[19] The Watchtower, *Bulletin*, October 1, 1920

prophets" foretell this? Sadly, instead of examining the Scriptures for what they actually say, many blindly went along with Rutherford's message.

On July 15, 1924, the Watchtower sent more material to reinforce their proclamation:

"The year 1925 is a date definitely and clearly marked in the Scriptures, even more than that of 1914."[20]

Again we must ask, where is 1914 or 1925 "marked?"

If this teaching wasn't bizarre enough, Rutherford went on to say, Abraham, Isaac, and Jacob would be resurrected in 1925 to represent God's new order of things on earth.

---

[20] *The Watchtower*, July 15, 1924, page 211

"millions now living will never die"

JUDGE RUTHERFORD

HIPPODROME

[21]"The chief thing to be restored is the human race to life; and since other Scriptures definitely fix the fact that there will be a resurrection of Abraham, Isaac, Jacob and other faithful ones of old, and that these will have the first favor, we may expect 1925 to witness the return of these faithful men of Israel from the condition of death, being resurrected and fully restored to perfect humanity and made the visible, legal representatives of the new order of things on earth."[22]

Rutherford went on to say,

---

[21] *The Sun and New York Herald*, March 20, 1920

[22] J. F. Rutherford, *Millions Now Living Will Never Die*, International Bible Students Association, Brooklyn NY, 1920, pages 88

"Therefore we may confidently expect that 1925 will mark the return of Abraham, Isaac, Jacob and the faithful prophets of old, particularly those named by the Apostle in Hebrews chapter eleven, to the condition of human perfection."[23]

Rutherford added some additional specifics to these prophecies, claiming Abraham, Isaac, and Jacob would be returning on or around April 1 of that year.

"…about April 1, 1925, at which time we may expect the resurrection of the Ancient Worthies."[24]

As you can expect, the ancient worthies did not come on April 1st 1925, nor did the world end that year. However, in expectation for these men of old, Rutherford built an immaculate mansion called Beth-Serim. The donations of Jehovah's Witnesses

---

[23] Ibid., pages 89-90
[24] Ibid., page 110

paid for this mansion so Abraham, Isaac, and Jacob would have a place to live when they come back to life.

When the Ancient Worthies failed to show up, the Watchtower found themselves with an empty mansion. But not all was lost. Conveniently, Judge Rutherford himself was able to take the mansion as his personal home.

Earthly Home For Israel King

Pictured is Rutherford with his 16-cylinder Fisher Fleetwood Cadillac coupe in front of Beth Serim.[25]

Another indicator that Rutherford was a false prophet is the simple fact that Jehovah's Witnesses have been dying. To put this prophecy into perspective, Rutherford's words ("Millions now living will never die") were penned over 100 years ago. For this prophecy to be accurate, there would

---

[25] Paul Grundy, JWFacts, *Beth-Sarim: House of Princes*, 2017, https://www.jwfacts.com/watchtower/bethsarim.php

have to be millions of 100-year-old Jehovah's Witnesses alive right now. We know this cannot be true because their numbers do not support such a demographic, proving it was a false prophecy.

Well, life went on for the Jehovah's Witnesses after 1925. The Watchtower made a few other predictions in the years to come, but none were emphasized more than that of 1975.

> "According to a more recent calculation of the Bible timetable, six thousand years of man's existence will end in the latter half of the year 1975, which is well within this century. The Bible millennium is ahead of us, and, according to the count of time and the events of world history, it is approaching."[26]

---

[26] *The Watchtower,* 1967 April 15, page 236

"Only a few years, at most, remain before the corrupt system of things dominating the earth is destroyed by God."[27]

Fear mongering was again, their favorite promotion method. The Watchtower explained how man's existence was destined to only last 6000 years and the dramatic end would take place in 1975.

[27] *Awake!*, October 8 1968, pages 14-15

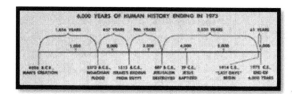

To support their prophecies, the Watchtower took quotes from well-known secular sources, including former U.S. Secretary of State Dean Acheson:

> "I know enough of what is going on to assure you that, in 15 years from today [or, by 1975], this world is going to be too dangerous to live in."[29]

Other fear mongering quotes include:

> "One of the greatest problems, beyond man's solving, is the coming food shortage due to the population explosion. In the book *Famine-1975!* Food experts W. and P.

---

[28] *Awake!,* October 8, 1968, page 15

[29] *Awake!,* October 8, 1968, page 15

Paddock state: 'By 1975 a disaster of unprecedented magnitude will face the world. Famines, greater than any in history, will ravage the undeveloped nations.' 'I forecast a specific date, 1975, when the new crisis will be upon us in all its awesome importance.' 'By 1975 civil disorder, anarchy, military dictatorships, runaway inflation, transportation breakdowns and chaotic unrest will be the order of the day in many of the hungry nations.'"[30]

Jehovah's Witnesses were so convinced by these end times prophecies that many quit their jobs and sold their homes. Farmers refused to plant so they could spend more time sharing Jehovah's message before the end.

As you can imagine, with all of this passion and urgency, the Watchtower saw record growth. But when 1975 turned out to be just another false

[30] *Awake!,* October 8, 1968, page 15

prophecy, many Jehovah's Witnesses became discouraged and left the organization, causing record drops in membership.

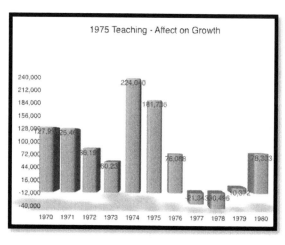

31

These are just a small sampling of the Watchtower's end times predictions. There is an abundance of this

31 JWfacts.com, *Facts About Jehovah's Witnesses, 1975 -* Watchtower Quotes, https://jwfacts.com/watchtower/1975.php

type of material that can be verified with the Watchtower's own sources. The organization inspired Jehovah's Witnesses with false prophecies in 1914, 1915, 1918, 1925, 1943, and 1975. Each time they stirred Witnesses to work a little harder and give a little more because "the end was just around the corner."

All of these proved to be false prophecies. 1975 was a wake-up call for many Jehovah's Witnesses. When these events failed to come true, 10% of their membership left. Sadly, the other 90% failed to reason objectively.

After all of these false end-times prophecies, we have to ask, did the Watchtower admit their errors? Did they ever ask Jehovah's Witnesses to forgive them for leading them astray so many years?

Not only did the Watchtower refuse confess their false doctrine, but shockingly, they diverted blame to the Jehovah's Witnesses themselves! The 1995 Awake magazine says,

wake!

False Predictions or True Prophecy
How Can You Tell the Difference?

"Bible Students, known since 1931 as Jehovah's Witnesses, also expected that the year 1925 would see the fulfillment of marvelous Bible prophecies. They surmised that at that time the earthly resurrection would begin, bringing back faithful men of old, such as Abraham, David, and Daniel. More recently, many Witnesses conjectured that events associated with the beginning of Christ's Millennial Reign might start to take place in 1975. Their anticipation was based on the understanding that the seventh millennium of human history would begin then."[32]

---

[32] *Awake!,* June 22, 1995, page 9

Friends, please listen to me. The Jehovah's Witnesses did not conjure up the idea that 1925 would be the end. Nor did they imagine men of old would come back that year. Nor did they invent the year of 1975 as being the end. They were repeatedly and consistently fed those ideas from the Watchtower!

Notice the Watchtower's wording about Jehovah's Witnesses, "They surmised" and "Witnesses conjectured" these events. To lie to Jehovah's Witnesses for over 50 years, and then try to pass the blame back on them is the worst kind of deceit and manipulation.

What's most disturbing about all of this is the Watchtower claimed to get their dates from the Bible. They were obviously extracting false information that one would never get from a conservative reading of Scripture.

Does this sound familiar? It should. They do the exact same thing when they say "Jesus is Michael the angel" or "Jesus should not be worshipped" or "hell is not real," etc. This is why we should read the Bible for what it plainly says instead of allowing an organization to force strange and bizarre doctrines upon us.

This journey through Watchtower material reveals that they have been *very* consistent in their teachings and predictions... consistently inconsistent! The fact that Jehovah's Witnesses continue to trust this organization is a testimony to the power of propaganda!

PART TWO

TWISTING THE SCRIPTURES

The Watchtower first published the New Testament of the New World Translation in 1950. In 1960, they completed the Old Testament and made the entire text available in 1961. The New World Translation was later revised in 1970, 1981, 1984, and 2013.

As of 2023, the Watchtower has printed 240 million copies of the New World Translation and it has been translated into at least 210 languages.[33] The English NWT was translated from Hebrew and

---

[33] JW.org, Jehovah's Witnesses, Online Bible, https://www.jw.org/en/library/bible/

Greek. Every translation after that was translated from English.

Perhaps more than any other Bible printed, the New

World Translation has faced tremendous criticism for a plethora of passages. Most people reading this translation may not pick up on these issues. After all, like any good piece of propaganda (or rat poison), 95% of it will be wholesome and good. But it is the 5% that will kill you.

The great majority of NWT verses are very much in line with the original Hebrew and Greek. However, other verses have subtle, and sometimes not-so-subtle differences that change the meaning of the text. Jehovah's Witnesses disagree. They believe the New World Translation is the most accurate Bible and that criticisms are merely the biased words of Trinitarians.

The next few chapters will leave absolutely no doubt where the bias lies.

Chapter Three

Giving Deception the Benefit of the Doubt

While it is easy to join the nay-sayers, I would like to give the Watchtower the benefit of the doubt in this chapter. Instead of casting judgement for everything that appears to be biased or contradictory, I would like to try to give them patience and understanding, refraining from criticism, even when the evidence and scholarship insist otherwise.

So, what are some of these alleged contradictions and biases? As we mentioned in an earlier chapter, the Watchtower instructed Jehovah's Witnesses to worship Jesus in the first half of their religion's existence. But later decided this was not a good idea, so they changed their minds.

It seems quite bizarre for a religion to make such a drastic shift in such a core doctrine. After all, the Watchtower is supposed to be the mouthpiece for Jehovah Himself. He is not one to change His mind on such things. Although I cannot think of any reasonable explanation for this, let's give the Jehovah's Witnesses the benefit of the doubt here. Let's assume they were justified in doing a complete 180 on their stance in Jesus worship.

So, what does the Bible have to say about Jesus receiving worship? To answer this, it all revolves around the Greek word, *proskuneo*.

This word is typically defined as "make obeisance [or] do reverence to." However, it is most frequently "rendered to worship."[34]

When the NWT translates the word "proskuneo" for Jesus, it uses the word "obeisance." The

[34] James Strong, *The New Strong's Expanded Exhaustive Concordance of the Bible Red-Letter Edition*, Thomas Nelson Publishers, Nashville, 2001, 4352

following are nine instances this word is found in the New World Translation in relation to Jesus:

- "We have come to do **obeisance** to him." (Matthew 2:2 NWT)
- "Report back to me so that I too may go and do **obeisance** to him." (Matthew 2:8 NWT)
- "They did **obeisance** to him." (Matthew 2:11 NWT)
- "Those in the boat did **obeisance** to him." (Matthew 14:33 NWT)
- "They approached and took hold of his feet and did **obeisance** to him." (Matthew 28:9 NWT)
- "When they saw him, they did **obeisance**." (Matthew 28:17 NWT)
- "They did **obeisance** to him." (Luke 24:52 NWT)
- "He said: "I do put faith in him, Lord." And he did **obeisance** to him." (John 9:38 NWT)

- "Let all of God's angels do **obeisance** to him." (Hebrews 1:6 NWT)

If you are anything like most people, you are probably asking, "What is obeisance?" This word means to give honor or show respect. It is not the same as worship. A man gives a high official or a king obeisance. A man gives God worship. Considering the definition of proskuneo, it is understandable why the Watchtower would choose to use this approach. After all, obeisance is part of the definition.

This leads us to ask, does any other Bibles use the word obeisance instead of worship? Looking at the English Standard version, it translates every one of these passages as worship:

- "…come to **worship** him." (Matthew 2:2 ESV)
- "…come and worship him." (Matthew 2:8 ESV)

- "...they fell down and **worshiped** him." (Matthew 2:11 ESV)
- "...those in the boat **worshiped** him" (Matthew 14:33 ESV)
- "they... took hold of his feet and **worshiped** him." (Matthew 28:9 ESV)
- "...they **worshiped** him." (Matthew 28:17 ESV)
- "...they **worshiped** him." (Luke 24:52 ESV)
- "He said, 'Lord, I believe,' and he **worshiped** him." (John 9:38 ESV)
- "Let all God's angels **worship** him." (Hebrews 1:6 ESV)

Looking through other reputable Bibles, the New American Standard Bible does the same thing. As does the King James. The New International Version also translated all these passages with "worship." As does the Revised Standard Version, the Amplified Bible, the New Living Translation, and the American Standard Version. In fact, every

Bible I can think of says the same thing: Jesus received worship. The only exception is the New World Translation.

This leaves us with only two possible scenarios:

1. The Watchtower's New World Translation is right, and all the Bibles ever translated throughout history are wrong.
2. The New World Translation is wrong and every other Bible is right.

This seems like incredible odds against the New World Translations. Although I cannot think of any reasonable explanation for this, let's give the Jehovah's Witnesses the benefit of the doubt here. Let's assume they were justified in doing a complete 180 on their stance in Jesus worship. Let's also assume the New World Translation has a more accurate rendering than every Bible ever written.

Perhaps the NWT is more consistent than any other Bible? After all, the Watchtower tells Jehovah's Witnesses that their text is the most accurate Bible and is written without bias. Let's take a look at this claim by exploring how the NWT translates the word "proskuneo" in other passages, particularly in passages addressing Jehovah. If the Watchtower is consistent, they should say Jehovah received obeisance as well.

- "It is Jehovah your God you must **worship**." (Matthew 4:10 NWT)
- "God is a Spirit, and those **worshipping** him must worship with spirit and truth." (John 4:24 NWT)
- "… fall facedown and **worship** God." (1 Corinthians 14:25 NWT)
- "For all the nations will come and **worship** before him." (Revelation 15:4 NWT)

In each of these passages, the Watchtower translates the word proskuneo as "worship." In fact, every time this word is applied to Jehovah, it is translated as worship. But every time it is applied to Jesus it is translated as obeisance. This does not look consistent. On one hand, the Watchtower claims it is consistent in its translations and refrains from using bias. But on the other hand, these passages seem to imply a lack of consistency and a lot of bias.

This too seems like incredible odds against the New World Translation. And although I cannot think of any reasonable explanation for this, let's give the Jehovah's Witnesses the benefit of the doubt here. Let's assume they were justified in doing a complete 180 on their stance in Jesus worship. Let's also assume the New World Translation is more accurate than every Bible ever written. And let's hope there is a good reason for these inconsistencies in translation between Jesus and Jehovah.

Perhaps the translators behind the NWT are superior to the thousands of Greek and Hebrew scholars who have ever translated the Bible? Maybe that is why their Bible is different. Let's take a look at the credentials of the New World Translation translators. After all, if they are superior in their Greek and Hebrew, perhaps they had good reason for applying the word "obeisance" to Jesus and not Jehovah.

So, who were the translators for the New World Translation? Interestingly, the Watchtower has always sought to keep their identity secret.

[35]Frederick W. Franz, former president of the Watchtower, testified to why the translators chose to be anonymous. In a 1954 Scottish court hearing, Franz was asked a series of questions:

"(Q) : Were you yourself responsible for the translation of the Old Testament?

(A) : Again I cannot answer that question...

---

[35]   Bible   Translation   and   Study, http://jehovah.to/xlation/fh.html

(Q): Why the secrecy?

(A): Because the committee of translation wanted it to remain anonymous and not seek any glory or honour at the making of a translation, and having any names attached thereto."[36]

There are serious issues with this stance. If we are not permitted to know who translated the New World Translation, how can we trust they had credentials to take on this task? We can't know if they were the most qualified men on the planet or if they were high school dropouts! Or worse yet, how are we to know if they even followed God? If the translators *were* qualified to take on this task, then the Watchtower's stance is not very helpful to those who wish to defend their translation.

---

[36] *Walsh Trial*, Internet Archive, Douglas Walsh v. The Right Honorable James Latham, Clyde, M.P., P.C., etc., Scotland, 1954, 1958 ed..p.92, https://archive.org/details/WalshTrial/page/n91/mode/2up

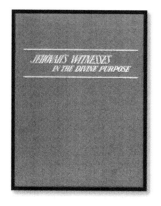

In addition to this, when asked "who were the ones on the committee that translated the Bible?" The Watchtower said, "The one request of the translation committee was that its members remain anonymous even after their death."[37]

This does not make a lot of sense, because many of the books of the Bible are literally named after their authors. These people were not seeking to get honor and they felt it was okay to identify themselves. Also, why would the translation committee request that their names remain secret after their death? How can they be tempted with pride after they are

---

[37] *Jehovah's Witnesses in the Divine Purpose*, Watch Tower Bible & Tract Society of Pennsylvania, Brooklyn NY, 1959, p. 258

already gone? These things seem unreasonable and I cannot think of any beneficial reason to take such a stance. If they were indeed competent translators, then let the world know. To keep these things secret only adds to the controversy and speculation. Many people believe the Watchtower strives to keep these names secret because the translators had no qualifications.

This appears to be a dark secret concerning the origins of the New World Translations. And although I cannot think of any reasonable explanation for this, let's give the Jehovah's Witnesses the benefit of the doubt here. Let's assume they were justified in doing a complete 180 on their stance in Jesus worship. Let's also assume the New World Translation is more accurate than every Bible ever written. Let's overlook their inconsistencies in translation between Jesus and Jehovah. Let's pretend their secret translation committee was the most godly, educated, and talented people to ever open the Bible.

Since the 1954 court hearing, there have been ex-Jehovah's Witnesses who divulged the names of the NWT translation committee. One of these individuals was former Governing Body member, Raymond Franz.

Franz wrote a book titled *Crisis of Conscious* where he testified to many of the behind-the-scenes activities of the governing body. He states the translators of the New World Translation were "Frederick W. Franz, Nathan A. Knorr, Gorge D. Gangas, Albert Schroeder, and Milton Henschel."[38] Researching these men show

---

[38] Raymond Franz, *Crisis of Conscience*, Fourth Edition, Commentary Press, Atlanta, 2004, page 56

that none of them were recognized Greek or Hebrew scholars.

Raymond Franz claimed that his uncle, Frederick W. Franz, was the only one who had "sufficient knowledge of the Bible languages to attempt translation of this kind. He had studied Greek for two years in the University of Cincinnati but was only self taught In Hebrew."[39]

In the 1954 Scotland trial, Frederick W. Franz, admitted that he was the person who confirmed the accuracy of the New World Translation.

The following is from the trial transcript: -

---

[39] Ibid., page 56

(Q): Insofar as translation of the Bible itself is undertaken, are you responsible for that?

(A): I have been authorized to examine a translation and determine its accuracy and recommend its acceptance in the form in which it is submitted.[40]

So, if a two-year Greek student/self-taught Hebrew student is the most qualified of the NWT translation committee, is it reasonable to trust them over all the

---

[40] *Walsh Trial*, Internet Archive, Douglas Walsh v. The Right Honorable James Latham
Clyde, M.P., P.C., etc., Scotland, 1954, 1958 ed., p.88, https://archive.org/details/WalshTrial/page/n91/mode/2up

teams of qualified scholars who have ever researched and deliberated over the Bible?

This seems like incredible odds against the New World Translation. And although I cannot think of any reasonable explanation for this, let's give the Watchtower the benefit of the doubt here. Let's assume they were justified in doing a complete 180 on their stance in Jesus worship. Let's also assume the New World Translation is more accurate than every Bible ever written. Let's hope there is a good reason for these inconsistencies in translations between Jesus and Jehovah. Let's pretend their secret translation committee was the most godly, educated, and talented people to ever open the Bible. And if Franz, Knorr, Gangas, Schroeder, and Henschel were the official committee, let's make believe this unscholarly group of men were superior to the thousands of Greek and Hebrew scholars who have ever translated the Bible.

I guess if we are willing to overlook all of these contradictions, biases, and controversies, then perhaps we are a good fit for the Watchtower and their doctrine.

Chapter Four

Hiding Jesus's Deity

One of the core teachings of the Watchtower is "Jesus is the Son of God, but He is not God Himself." This stance has caused no small disagreement with Greek and Hebrew scholars.

Many theologians' accuse the Watchtower of adjusting the New World Translation to fit their doctrine instead of allowing their doctrine to fit the Bible. The following is an overview of the main Scriptures in question.

John 1:1

"In the beginning was the Word, and the Word was with God, and the Word was **a god**." (John 1:1 NWT)

"In the beginning was the Word, and the Word was with God, and the Word was **<u>God</u>**." (John 1:1 ESV)

The key difference between these two translations is the identity of the Word (Jesus). The English Standard Version, as well as the majority of other Bibles, identifies Jesus as "God" while the New World Translation identifies Jesus as "a god." It is hard to underestimate the significance here. One side claims Jesus is the Almighty God of the universe while the other side claims Jesus is merely a lesser god.

The Greek word for "God" in this passage is "*theon*." The New World Translation adheres to the rendering Jesus is "a god" because there is no definite article preceding theon. The Watchtower maintains, if the definite article would have been in the text, it would read "the God," but since the definite article is missing, it remains "a god." This is taught with much emphasis throughout Jehovah's Witness communities.

In contrast to this, the majority of other Bibles translate "theon" as "God" because the definite article is not always needed in the Greek language. Greek scholar Rudolph Gonzalez says it this way:

> "Colwell's rule: Definite predicate nouns, which proceed the verb usually lack the article... such predicate nouns are normally qualitative, sometimes definite, rarely indefinite. In all cases, context is the determinant factor."[41]

This explanation has been known for many years even though Watchtower translators remain steadfast with their rule. However, there is an issue with their consistency. The Watchtower is

[41] Rudolph Gonzalez, *The New World Translation Under the Lens of Biblical Greek*, Oct 22, 2019, https://www.youtube.com/watch?v=wd398oz_HLE

passionate about the missing article in John 1:1, but have no problem breaking their rule when it goes against their doctrine. For example, the word "theon" is used repeatedly by John, often without the definite article. John 1:18 actually uses it twice, both times without the definite article. Watchtower translators find themselves in a difficult position because calling them both "a god" would force them to call Jehovah "a god." And if they decide to call them both "God," the Watchtower would find itself calling Jesus "God." Neither of these is acceptable in Watchtower doctrine, so they decide to split the difference by saying theon is "God" once and "a god" once.

> "No man has seen **God** at any time; the only-begotten **god** who is at the Father's side." (John 1:18 NWT)

> "No one has ever seen **God**; the only **God**, who is at the Father's side." (John 1:18 ESV)

Again the New World Translation makes a distinction between God and Jesus while the English Standard Version claims they are both "God." Had the Watchtower maintained their rule, they would have to call both the Father and the Son "a god."

The lack of a definite article is not the only problem surrounding the NWT's rendering of John 1:1. The translation "a god" also appears to contradict the Bible's unified Monotheistic message. Bruce Metzger, professor of New Testament language and literature at Princeton Theological Seminary rightfully points out that "if the Jehovah's Witnesses take this translation seriously, they are polytheists."[42] To say there is a second god contradicts other sections of Scripture. For example:

[42] Bruce M. Metzger, *The Jehovah's Witnesses and Jesus Christ: A Biblical and Theological Appraisal*, Theology Today 10/1, April 1953, pp. 65-85

"I am the first and I am the last; besides me there is no god… you are my witnesses! Is there a God besides me?" There is no Rock; I know not any." (Isaiah 44:6, 8 ESV)

A key person in the New World Translation's use of "a god" is a man named Johannes Greber. Greber translated his own version of the New Testament and the Watchtower used him on several occasions as their "reputable" source, particularly for John 1:1. His quotes supporting this verse can be found in the following Watchtower publications:

- *The Word-Who is He? - According to John*, 1962, page 5

- *The Watchtower*, September 15, 1962, page 554

- *Make Sure of All Things Hold Fast to What is Fine*, 1965, page 489

- *Aid to Bible Understanding*, 1971, pg. 1669

The issue arises when one discovers how Greber translated his Bible. The preface of his New Testament reveals some disturbing information:

"The New Testament, as interpreted by the scholarly Pastor Johannes Greber, has as its source the oldest manuscripts in the world, made available to Pastor Greber for study and translation through the courtesy and cooperation of theological experts and museums the world over. This is an absolutely independent translation, without restriction to the dogma of any Church. The task was not simple. Many

67

contradictions between what appears in the ancient scrolls and the New Testament, as we have grown to know it, arose and were the subject of his constant prayers for guidance — prayers that were answered, and the discrepancies clarified to him, by God's Spirit World. At times he was given the correct answers in large illuminated letters and words passing before his eyes. Other times he was given the correct answers during prayer meetings. His wife, a medium of God's Spirit world was often instrumental in conveying the correct answers from God's Messengers to Pastor Greber."[43]

Translating a text is typically a scholarly work, but it is understandable why a Christian would commit difficult texts to prayer. However, receiving

---

[43] Johannes Greber, *New Testament English Translation*, 1937, Preface

translations from a medium is a serious matter. Mixing the work of God with the occult is never an acceptable practice. Greber himself wrote a book called *Communication with the Spirit World of God*.

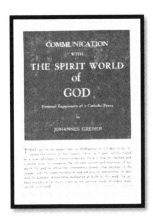

Using a questionable "scholar" like Johannes Greber was enough to send shockwaves of distrust throughout Jehovah's Witness circles. But ironically, it was the Watchtower's use of credible Greek scholars that may have exposed their deceit even more than Greber's spiritualism.

The Watchtower used the quotes of Julius Mantey (President of International Greek Research) in their

Kingdom Interlinear to support their translation of John 1:1.[44]

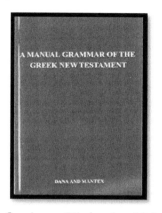

It's understandable why the Watchtower would want to quote Mantey. He was considered one of the top Greek scholars of the 20th century. He was the professor of New Testament and Greek at Northern Seminary. His book, *A Manual Grammar of the Greek New Testament* was utilized as a text book in numerous seminaries for over 60 years.

The problem is the Watchtower quoted Mantey as support for their rendition even though he opposed

---

44 The Watchtower, *The Kingdom Interlinear Translation of the Greek Scriptures*, 1969 edition, pp. 1158, 1159

it! When Mantey discovered how the Watchtower quoted him, he wrote a scathing response:

"Theos on John 1:1 is not indefinite and should not be translated 'a god'. Watchtower writers appear to be the only ones advocating such a translation… You have been quoting me out of context, I herewith request you not to quote the *Manuel Grammar of the Greek New Testament* again, which you have been doing for 24 years. Also, that you not quote it or me in

45 https://rispondiaitdg.altervista.org/wp-content/uploads/2021/06/Lettera-di-Julius-Mantey.pdf

any of your publications from this time on."[46]

"There is no statement in our grammar that was ever meant to imply that "a god" was a permissible translation in John 1:1."[47]

Mantey had more to say about the Watchtower and their literature. In one interview, Mantey held up some Watchtower literature and said,

"I have never found any so-called translation that goes so far away from what the Scripture actually teaches as these books published by Jehovah's Witnesses. They are so far away from what there is in the original Hebrew and the original Greek... It's because they're so biased and

---

[46] Julius Mantey, *A letter addressed to the Watchtower Bible and Tract Society*, July 11, 1974
[47] Ibid.

deceptive. Because they deliberately changed words in the passage of Scripture to make it fit into their doctrine. They distorted the Scripture in many passages, scores and scores of passages in the New Testament dealing with the deity of Christ especially."[48]

The Watchtower did not learn from this sharp reprimand. Eight years later they misquoted another famous Greek scholar named William Barclay.

Their May 15, 1977 Watchtower magazine[49] claimed that Barclay supported their view of John 1:1.

---

[48] Jeremiah Films, *Witnesses of Jehovah - Complete Official*, 2012, https://www.youtube.com/watch?v=VE3zp9FiyiQ

[49] The Watchtower, May 15, 1977, page 320

"When Dr. Barclay saw what had been published in The Watchtower, he wrote a reply: 'The Watchtower article has, by judicious cutting, made me say the opposite of what I meant to say.'"[50]

It is unlikely that the New World Translation will be changing their rendition of John 1:1 anytime soon, but this mistranslation can be quickly exposed if readers would only adhere to reputable and trustworthy sources.

John 8:58

"Jesus said to them: 'Most truly I say to you, before Abraham came into existence, **I have been.**'" (John 8:58 NWT)

"Truly, truly, I say to you, before Abraham was, **I am**." (John 8:58 ESV)

---

[50] Randall Watters, *Thus Saith… the Governing Body of Jehovah's Witnesses*, Manhattan Beach, CA, Bethel Ministries, 1984, pages 72-74

The New World Translation claims this passage refers to Jesus' age. By translating John 8:58 as "I have been," they are reinforcing the Watchtower's doctrine that Jesus is a created being. The English Standard Version, as well as most other Bibles, translates this text, "I am," making the direct connection to Exodus 3:14, where God said to Moses at the burning bush, "I am who I am." In other words, Jesus is telling the Jews in John 8:58, "I am God almighty."

It is obvious that the Jews were not naïve to what Jesus was saying because the next verse says, "they picked up stones to throw at him, but Jesus hid himself and went out of the temple." (John 8:59 ESV) If Jesus was simply stating He was very old, as the Watchtower claims, the Jews would have likely mocked Him, labeling Him a crazy person. On the other hand, identifying Himself as God in the flesh was a serious offense for these pious Jews. The Torah instructs: "Whoever blasphemes the name of the Lord shall surely be put to death. All the congregation shall stone him." (Leviticus 24:16 ESV) The Jews' reaction shows they were attempting to fulfill this command because Jesus calling Himself with God.

> "The words in question are "*ego eimi*" which mean, 'I am.' The New World Translation attempts to change John 8:58 by claiming that ego eimi should be translated with a perfect verb, but the reality is, it should be translated as a present, active, indicative. There is not grammatical basis for [the Watchtower's] change."[51]

In an attempt to justify their translation, the Watchtower inserted a footnote into their 1950 New World Translation, explaining why they used

---

[51] Rudolph Gonzalez, *The New World Translation Under the Lens of Biblical Greek*, Oct 22, 2019, https://www.youtube.com/watch?v=wd398oz_HLE

"I have been" instead of "I am." This footnote claims that the Greek for John 8:58 "is rendered in the perfect indefinite tense."

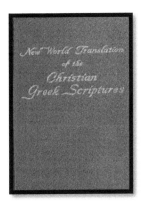

Interestingly, the perfect indefinite tense does not exist in Greek or any other language. The Watchtower totally made the term up! It did not take long for scholars to object to this fallacy, so the Watchtower changed their explanation to something else. With such a lack of integrity, it becomes obvious why this translation is viewed with suspicion.

Colossians 1:16-17

"because by means of him **all other things** were created in the heavens and on the earth, the things visible and the things invisible, whether they are thrones or lordships or governments or authorities. **All other things** have been created through him and for him. Also, he is before **all other things**, and by means of him **all other things** were made to exist." (Colossians 1:16-17 NWT)

"For by him **all things** were created, in heaven and on earth, visible and invisible, whether thrones or dominions or rulers or authorities—**all things** were created through him and for him. And he is before

all things, and in him **all things** hold together." (Colossians 1:16-17 ESV)

In what may be the most blatant and unprecedented addition to Scripture, the New World Translation goes out of its way to hide Jesus' deity by adding the word "other" four times to the above passage. The Watchtower's agenda for doing this is to support their claim that Jesus is a created being. The original manuscripts do not contain anything resembling the word "other." On the contrary, the passage clearly says that Jesus created "all things" and that He is before "all things." And since only God could have created all things, this means Colossians 1:16-17 is calling Jesus the Almighty God of the universe. This obviously contradicts Watchtower doctrine, so they decided to add the word "other" to make it sound like Jesus was Jehovah's first creation.

How can the Watchtower justify such corruption? For them, this is permissible because of how they view the context. The prior verse reads:

"He is the image of the invisible God, the firstborn of all creation." (Colossians 1:15 ESV)

The Watchtower understands the title "firstborn" to mean Jesus is created. And if He was the first creation, then this must mean that Jesus created everything else, hence, all "other" things. However, there are several problems with this interpretation.

The question must be asked, if Paul is trying to say Jesus was the first of God's creations, why did he choose to use the word "firstborn," instead of "first creation"? To answer this, one must examine how the term "firstborn" was used in other places in the Bible.

David was called the "firstborn" in Psalm 89:27. But how could he be firstborn when it is common knowledge David was the lastborn of Jesse? Israel was also called "firstborn" in Exodus 4:22. But how can a nation be firstborn; especially a nation that came so much later than other nations?

To answer this, the term "firstborn" means preeminent one or the one with supremacy. In other words, this term refers to Jesus as first in rank. It does not mean that He was created. Bruce Metzger agrees,

> "First begotten of all creation... is something quite different from saying that he was made or created. If Paul had wished to express the latter idea, he had available a Greek word to do so, the word, *protoktistos,* meaning 'first created.' Actually, however, Paul uses the word, *prototokos,* meaning 'first begotten,' which signifies something quite different."[52]

---

[52] Bruce Metzger, *Theology Today*, v. 10, April 1953 page 76-77

It might be worth noting that Metzger has been labeled the greatest New Testament scholar to ever come out of North America. The context supports his interpretation. Looking at verse 18:

> "And **he is the head** of the body, the church. He is the beginning, the firstborn from the dead, that in everything he might be **preeminent.**" (Colossians 1:18 ESV)

Who other than the supreme, first in rank, preeminent God can be the Creator of "all things"? A proper understanding of Jesus is that He is the begotten Son of God, not the created Son of God. C.S. Lewis provides further understanding between the terms begotten and created:

> "We don't use the word begotten much in modern English, but everyone still knows what it means. To beget is to become the father of. To create is to make. And the difference is just this. When you beget, you

beget something of the same kind as yourself. Here are a few examples to illustrate:

A bird creates a nest.

A beaver creates a dam.

A man creates a house.

God creates man.

A bird begets a bird.

A beaver begets a beaver.

A man begets a man.

God begets God."[53]

[53] C.S. Lewis, *Mere Christianity*, 1952, Harper Collins Publishers, pages 129-130

The Watchtower is not quick to accept this, so they try to apply Proverbs 8 to Jesus, claiming He is the first of Jehovah's acts:

> "The Lord possessed me at the beginning of his work, the first of his acts of old. Ages ago I was set up, at the first, before the beginning of the earth… then I was beside him, like a master workman, and I was daily his delight, rejoicing before him always." (Proverbs 8:22-23, 30 ESV)

Reading the context of this passage, the one speaking is God's wisdom and it is being referred to as a "master workman." In Watchtower doctrine, the master workman in this passage is Jesus, who is called the "first of his acts" and was set up "ages ago." With this mindset, it is understandable why Jehovah's Witnesses assume Jesus is created, but again, this does not fit the narrative for several reasons:

For starters, we cannot automatically assume the wisdom in this chapter is Jesus simply because it never identifies Him by name or person. Another obvious reason is if Jesus is the wisdom in this chapter, it would insinuate that Jehovah does not have wisdom of His own. But the most compelling reason Jesus is not a creation is found in the book of Isaiah:

> "I am the LORD, who made all things, **who alone** stretched out the heavens, who spread out the earth **by myself**," (Isaiah 44:24 ESV)

Jehovah says that He is the Maker of all things and He had *no* help. Watchtower doctrine contradicts this by saying Jesus made everything except Himself. The true reading of Colossians 1:16 says that Jesus was the Creator of "all things." So how can one reconcile Isaiah 44:24 and Colossians 1:16? The answer is simple, Jehovah and Jesus are the same God, just like John 1:1, John 8:58, Titus 2:13, and Hebrews 1:8 says!

Adding words to the Bible in order to make Jesus some kind of creation, causes contradiction in other areas. If the Bible says Jesus created "all things," it would be wrong to tell people He didn't. Colossians 1:16-17 is not the only place the Watchtower adds the word "other" to the Bible. They practice the same principle for Philippians 2:9.

> "For this very reason, God exalted him to a superior position and kindly gave him the name that is above **every other** name." (Philippians 2:9 NWT)

> "Therefore God has highly exalted him and bestowed on him the name that is above **every** name" (Philippians 2:9 ESV)

The Watchtower knows they cannot leave the name of Jesus above *all* names. If they did, it would communicate that He is God, so they added the word "other" to justify their theology. No other Bible has the word "other" in these texts. Neither does the Greek. It was biasedly added to sway the reader to adopt their doctrine.

Titus 2:13

"while we wait for the happy hope and glorious manifestation of the great God and **of** our Savior, Jesus Christ," (Titus 2:13 NWT)

"waiting for our blessed hope, the appearing of the glory of our great God and Savior Jesus Christ," (Titus 2:13 ESV)

In a very subtle way, the New World Translation hides Jesus' deity by adding the word "of." Without the word "of," this passage clearly describes God and Jesus Christ as the same. But with the word "of," this passage speaks as if God and Jesus are separate. As with many other passages describing Jesus' deity, the New World Translation is the only

Bible that adds this extra word. Bruce Metzger explains why the New World Translation is in error with Titus 2:13:

> "This rendering, by separating "the great God" from "our Savior Christ Jesus," overlooks a principle of Greek grammar which was detected and formulated in a rule by Granville Sharp in 1798. This rule, in brief, is that when the copulative καί connects two nouns of the same case, if the article precedes the first noun and is not repeated before the second noun, the latter always refers to the same person that is expressed or described by the first noun. This verse in Titus, therefore, must be translated, as in fact the Revised Standard Version renders it, 'Awaiting our blessed hope, the appearing of the glory of our great God and Savior Jesus Christ.' In support of this translation, there may be

quoted such eminent grammarians of the Greek New Testament as P. W. Schmiedel, J. H. Moulton, A. T. Robertson, and Blass-Debrunner. All of these scholars concur in the judgment that only one person is referred to in Titus 2:13 and that therefore it must be rendered, 'Our great God and Savior Jesus Christ.'"[54]

Those who do not read Greek can also confirm the translation of this passage. Three verses earlier in Titus 2:10, the reader is given solid evidence why verse 13 calls God and Jesus the same person:

"...so that in everything they may adorn the doctrine of **God our Savior**." (Titus 2:10 NIV)

---

[54] Bruce M. Metzger, *The Jehovah's Witnesses and Jesus Christ: A Biblical and Theological Appraisal*, Theology Today 10/1, April 1953, pages 65-85

This passage calls God "our Savior" and verse 13 calls Jesus "our Savior." This throws mixed messages with the New World Translation's attempt to separate God and Jesus, but this makes perfect sense with every other Bible rendition that calls Jesus "God."

Hebrews 1:8

"But about the Son, he says: '**God is your throne** forever and ever.'" (Hebrews 1:8 NWT)

"But of the Son he says, '**Your throne, O God**, will last for ever and ever.'" (Hebrews 1:8 ESV)

Looking at the context of this verse, the writer of Hebrews says Jesus is:

- "the heir of all things" (Heb. 1:2)
- "maker of the universe" (Heb. 1:2)
- "God's exact representation" (Heb. 1:3)

- "He sustains all things by His powerful word" (Heb. 1:3)
- "He is superior to all the angels" (Heb. 1:4)
- "all the angels worship Him" (Heb. 1:6)

The writer of Hebrews used all these descriptions to say, Jesus is God without actually saying "Jesus is God." But then, to make sure there is no doubt, the writer just comes out and says it in verse 8!

This is where the New World Translation plays an interesting trick. In their attempt to avoid calling Jesus "God," the Watchtower switches the words around to say "God is your throne" instead of "Your throne, O God."

There are at least two issues with this rendering. For one, the term "God is your throne" is a confusing statement that doesn't even make sense. The other problem is that Hebrews 1:8 is a direct quote from Psalms 45:6:

"**Your throne, O God**, is forever and ever." (Psalms 45:6 ESV)

The Psalmist is specifically referring to Jehovah here. So when the writer of Hebrews applies this passage to Jesus, he is plainly stating, "Jesus and Jehovah are the same God." The only way to avoid this conclusion is to unjustifiably switch the words around, just as the New World Translation has done.

Just about every Bible commentary supports calling Jesus "God" in Hebrews 1:8. Jehovah's Witnesses attempt to challenge this information with three arguments:

1. "Almost every Bible Commentary that has been written is Trinitarian, so of course they are going to translate this text that way."

2. "The New World Translation is not alone in Hebrews 1:8. The James Moffatt

Translation and the American Translation also use the term 'God is your throne.'"

3. The context of Psalm 45:6 is referring to an earthly king, not God.

Addressing these arguments one at a time, it is true almost every Bible Commentary is Trinitarian. But why do you suppose that is? When we look at the folks who write Bible commentaries, they are typically some of the most educated individuals on the planet. They are men and women who have spent countless years gaining Masters and Doctorate degrees so they can be equipped to commentate on the Bible. So, when almost all of these Biblically educated people are Trinitarian, that in itself should tell us something. It should tell us the Bible is Trinitarian! It's just as simple as that. There are just too many passages that testify to the doctrine of the Trinity.

The second rebuttal of Jehovah's Witnesses is that two other Bibles give the same rendering for

Hebrews 1:8, the James Moffatt Translation and the American Translation.

It is also true that these Bibles give a similar rendering as the New World Translation, but the question is, why? Of all the different Bibles that disagree with the NWT, why are there two translations that agree?

To answer this, it is first important to understand that behind most Bible translations, there is a translation team. About 40 to 100 scholars get together to work on translating the Greek and Hebrew. These men and women debate, haggle, and collaborate over passages until they come to a conclusion that gives justice to the text. Many ideas get rejected in this process. That is why it is important to have a variety of scholars working on these projects.

This being said, do you know how many people worked on the James Moffatt Translation? There weren't 40 -100 scholars. It was... James Moffatt!

James Moffatt came out with his own translation of the Bible. It was the work of one man, and there was no one holding him accountable to his ideas.

Friends, this is what I want you to consider: I can also create my own Bible. And as I translate I can add anything I want to the Bible. I can claim something stupid like "Peter and James ate pork nine times every day" and then add that to the New Testament. Who's going to stop me? Who is going to collaborate with me? Who is going to ask me, "Where in the world are you getting this translation?!"

So, yes, James Moffatt wrote a translation that also said, "God is your throne," but he had no one holding him accountable. And if he was off on some heretical bend in his theology, there was no one to stop him.

When we look at the American Translation, it was written by Edgar Goodspeed and J.M. Powis Smith.

When we look at this translation, there weren't 40-100 people working on it. There was only Goodspeed and Smith.

So, yes! There are two other Bibles that also use the translation "God is your throne," but it is basically the opinions of three men!

Down this same line of thinking, anyone else could write a Bible using the phrase, "God is your throne." He could then get his Bible published and put it on the shelf for people to buy. Then the Jehovah's Witnesses could add a third translation to their list of Bibles that teach fallacy and heresy!

As for the last of the Jehovah's Witness rebuttals, "the context of Psalm 45:6 is not about God, it's about an earthly king." To this I simply like to ask the question, "Okay, if this passage is about an earthly king, who was the king?"

I ask this for an important reason. The Jehovah's Witnesses say, "look at the context." Well, when we look at the context, it is talking about an extraordinary king. In fact, this king is so amazing, verse 17 says,

"I will cause your name to be remembered in all generations; therefore nations will praise you forever and ever." (Psalm 45:17 ESV)

This king's name will be remembered for all generations, so I ask the Jehovah's Witnesses,

"What's the king's name?"

No response.

"Come on! The Bible clearly tells us this king's name is famous and it will never be forgotten! So, what is his name?"

Again, no response.

"This name is supposed to be remembered in all generations, including our generation. So, if you do not know the name, then there must be something wrong!"

When we ask the Jews, "Who is the king in Psalm 45?" They respond by saying, "He is the Messiah."

This is where we can refute a Jew and a Jehovah's Witness at the same time. One group will claim this person is a king and the other group will claim he is the Messiah, but neither will give you a name. But the Bible says, "His name will be remembered!"

Halleluiah! His name is remembered. His name is Jesus! He is the King of Kings and the Lord of Lords. He is God in the flesh who came and died to make satisfaction for our sins. He is the one who is and was and will be. He is the one every knee will bow to. He is our God and our king and His throne is forever and ever!

Chapter Five

The Cross and the Torture Stake

"Whoever does not carry his **<u>torture stake</u>** and come after me cannot be my disciple." (Luke 14:27 NWT)

"Whoever does not bear his own **<u>cross</u>** and come after me cannot be my disciple." (Luke 14:27 ESV)

The Watchtower is very passionate about the shape of the Roman torture device. They insist that instead of a cross, Jesus was killed on an upright stake. Because of this belief, everywhere the word "cross" is found in the New Testament, the New World Translation replaces it with the words "torture stake."

As with many other Watchtower teachings, they used to teach the exact opposite of what they hold to today. In 1914, Charles Taze Russell made a photo drama of creation. In it he pictured Jesus dying on the cross, not a stake.

55

56

---

55 *A 100-Year-Old Epic of Faith*, JW.org, https://www.jw.org/en/library/magazines/w20140215/photo-drama-of-creation/

56 *The Photo Drama of Creation*, slide 65

Judge Rutherford also taught that Jesus died on a cross, as pictured here in the Harp of God.

The teaching of the cross was so prominent in early Watchtower doctrine that it was used as an identifier and placed on the upper left hand corner of their magazines.

---

[57] J.F. Rutherford, *Harp of God*, Watch Tower Bible and Tract Society, Brooklyn NY, 1921, page 112

The October 1st 1931 Watchtower (pictured center) was the last time the cross appeared on the cover of their magazine. The October 15th 1931 (pictured right) shows the magazine without the cross.

So, why did the Watchtower make such a change in their doctrine? They did this for two reasons.

1. The Greek word in question is "stauros" and the Watchtower claims that this should be translated as "torture stake."

2. The Watchtower teaches that the idea of Jesus dying on a cross originated in the 3rd century with the Roman Emperor Constantine. They claim Rome was having internal struggles, so Constantine tried to

make peace by blending Christian practices with pagan practices. One of these compromises was to replace the torture stake with the cross that represented the Chaldean god Tammuz.

An unbiased study of Greek and ancient history tells a different story. The following Greek source provides examples of four different crosses used in execution:

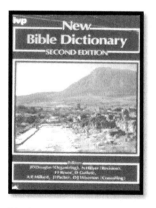

"The Gk. word for 'cross' (stauros; verb stauroō; Lat. crux, crucifigo) means primarily an upright stake or beam, and secondarily a stake used as an instrument for punishment and execution. It is used in this latter sense in the NT.... Apart from the single upright post (crux simplex) on which the victim was tied or impaled, there were three types of cross. The crux commissa (St Anthony's cross) was shaped like a capital T, thought by some to be derived from the symbol of the god Tammuz, the letter tau; the crux decussata (St Andrew's cross was shaped like the letter X; the crux immissa was the familiar two beams †, held by tradition to be the shape of the cross on which our Lord died (Irenaeus, Haer. 2.24.4). This is strengthened by the references in the four Gospels (Mt. 27:37; Mk. 15:26; Lk. 23:38; Jn 19:19-22) to the title nailed to the cross of Christ over his head."[58]

After reading the descriptions of these four versions of stauros, it is clear that this source supports the evidence that Jesus died on the traditional "†" shaped cross. The Watchtower quoted this same source in their publication, *Insight on the Scriptures*. However, in what appears to be their normal practice, the Watchtower strategically cut sections

[58] J. B. T., *"Cross, Crucifixion,"* New Bible Dictionary, ed. J. D. Douglas, 2nd ed. Leicester, England: Inter-Varsity Press, p. 253

out, forcing this text to say the opposite of what it intended to say:

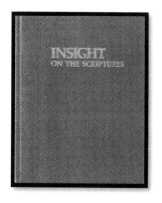

"Stau·ros' in both the classical Greek and Koine carries no thought of a "cross" made of two timbers. It means only an upright stake, pale, pile, or pole, as might be used for a fence, stockade, or palisade. Says Douglas' New Bible Dictionary of 1985 under "Cross," page 253: 'The Gk. word for 'cross' (stauros; verb stauroo…) means primarily an upright stake or beam, and secondarily a stake used as an instrument for punishment and execution.'"[59]

Examples like these should be disturbing to readers of Watchtower material. The problem is, most

---

[59] Watchtower, "Impalement," *Insight on the Scriptures*, 1988), 1:1191, ellipsis in original

Jehovah's Witnesses fail to investigate what they are being taught because the Watchtower instructs them to be suspicious of outside publications. So, even though this fallacy is simple to trace, the Watchtower knows most Jehovah's Witnesses will probably never see it.

A study of the Bible and church history explains why Christians believe Jesus died on a cross and that it did not originate with 3rd-century pagan worship. The Bible provides two clues that support a "✝" shaped cross. The first is found in the Gospel of Matthew. It says that after Jesus was crucified, they placed a sign "over his head." (Matthew 27:37) Had it been a torture stake, Jesus' hands would have been over his head and the passage would have read, they placed a sign "over his hands."

The other clue from the Bible comes from John's Gospel:

> "So the other disciples told him, 'We have
> seen the Lord.' But [Thomas] said to them,
> 'Unless I see in his hands the mark of the
> **nails**, and place my finger into the mark of

60   *The Ransom – God's Greatest Gift*, JW.org, https://www.jw.org/en/library/books/bible-teach/the-ransom-jesus-sacrifice/

61   *Svitozar Nenyuk, fineartamerica*, https://fineartamerica.com/featured/jesus-christ-on-the-cross-crucifixion-svitozar-nenyuk.html

the **nails**, and place my hand into his side,
I will never believe.'" (John 20:25 ESV)

John uses the plural for nails when he says, "where the nails were." Had Jesus died on a stake, there would have been one nail (singular) that went through both of His hands. But on a cross, Jesus' hands would have been outstretched and nails (plural) would have been driven through each hand separately.

Church history provides further evidence that the cross did not originate in the third century. In 160 A.D., Justin Martyr described the cross:

"...one beam is placed upright, from which the highest extremity is raised up into a horn, when the other beam is fitted on to it, and the ends appear on both sides as horns joined on to the one horn. And the part which is fixed in the center, on which are suspended those who are crucified."[62]

In 180 A.D., Irenaeus likewise described the cross:

"The very form of the cross, too, has five extremities, two in length, two in breadth, and one in the middle, on which… the person rests who is fixed by the nails."[63]

[64]Sometime around the 2nd-century, the Alexamenos Graffito was engraved on a wall depicting "a human-like figure who is attached to a cross and who has the head of a donkey. To the left of the image is a young man, apparently

---

[62] Justin Martyr, *Dialogue with Trypho*, CXI

[63] Irenaeus, *Against Heresies*, Book II Chapter 24

[64] *Bethinking, Artistic Response to the Cross Throughout History*, https://www.bethinking.org/culture/artistic-responses-cross

intended to represent Alexamenos, who is raising one hand in a gesture possibly suggesting worship. Beneath the cross there is a caption written in Greek: Αλεξαμενος cεβετε θεον, which means Alexamenos worships God."[65]

Although this image was originally used to mock Christians, it is strong evidence Jesus died on a cross and that believers worshipped Him as God before the time of Constantine.

It becomes very difficult to trust the New World Translation's usage of the term "torture stake" when the reader takes the time to compare the usage of the Greek word "stauros, the Biblical clues, the evidence of Church history, and the deceptive quoting of the Watchtower.

---

[65] Trevor Allin, *Did Christ Die on a Cross or a Stake*, 2017, http://livingwater-spain.com/crucfixn.pdf

Chapter Six

Is God "Jehovah" or is He "Lord"?

If you have ever discussed the New World Translation with a Jehovah's Witness, you have probably heard them say one of two things:

1. "The New World Translation is the most accurate Bible because it is void of bias."
2. "The New World Translation restores the name "Jehovah" to the Bible."

The Watchtower teaches that it is only proper to call God by His name, not His title. The name Jehovah originates from the Hebrew Tetragrammaton (YHWH). This is often translated into Greek as "kurios." The Watchtower claims that most Bibles have removed the name "Jehovah" and wrongfully replaced it with the title "Lord."

66

The exact pronunciation of the Tetragrammaton is unknown. Many scholars believe "Yahweh" is the most accurate way to say this name, but few have any real issue with the use of the name Jehovah. However, there are serious inconsistencies with when the New World Translation decides to use this name and when it does not. One problem text is found in Paul's quoting of Isaiah 45.

> "By myself I have sworn; The word has
> gone out of my mouth in righteousness,

---

66   *Yahweh   is   My   Shepherd,*
http://myheavenlyhome.blogspot.com/2010/12/yahwehs-name-identifies-his-people.html

113

And it will not return: To me every knee will bend, Every tongue will swear loyalty." (Isaiah 45:23 NWT)

There is no denying that God is the subject in this passage and it clearly explains that every knee will bow to Him. The Apostle Paul quotes this passage two times in the New Testament. The first is Romans 14:11.

"For it is written: 'As surely as I live,' says **Jehovah**, 'to me every knee will bend, and every tongue will make open acknowledgment to God.'" (Romans 14:11 NWT)

Paul chose the word "kurios" for his quoting of Isaiah 45:23. The NWT translates this word as "Jehovah." The second time Paul quotes Isaiah 45:23 is in Philippians 2:10-11.

"so that in the name of Jesus every knee should bend—of those in heaven and those on earth and those under the ground and every tongue should openly acknowledge that Jesus Christ is **Lord** to the glory of God the Father." (Philippians 2:10-11 NWT)

Here Paul is quoting the same Old Testament passage with the exact same Greek word (kurios). But the NWT translates one as "Jehovah" and the other as "Lord" because they refuse to call Jesus God. This is a biased way to translate.

Another example of this type of inconsistency is in comparing Psalms 102 and Hebrew 1:

"I said: "O my **God**, Do not do away with me in the middle of my life, You whose years span all generations. Long ago you laid the foundations of the earth, And the heavens are the work of your hands." (Psalms 102:24-25 NWT)

The Psalmist is referring to God. The writer of Hebrews quotes this same passage, again, using the Greek word "kurios." For the New World

Translation to stay consistent, they would have to translate this word as "God," but since the writer of Hebrews is applying this passage to Jesus, the NWT conveniently uses the word "Lord."

> "At the beginning, O **Lord**, you laid the foundations of the earth, and the heavens are the works of your hands." (Hebrews 1:10 NWT)

The Watchtower spends a lot of time and resources discrediting other Bibles for using the title "Lord" in place of YHWH and kurios. However, it is important to note that other Bibles are consistent in their translation of these words. The New World Translation claims to "bring back" God's name by translating YHWH and kurios as Jehovah, however, they are inconsistent with their own translation rule so they can avoid calling Jesus "God." This contradicts the Watchtower's other claim that the New World Translation is void of bias.

Chapter Seven

Withholding the Evidence for Hell

"And if your eye makes you stumble, throw it away. It is better for you to enter one-eyed into the Kingdom of God than to be thrown with two eyes into **Ge·hen′na**," (Mark 9:47 NWT)

"And if your eye causes you to sin, tear it out. It is better for you to enter the kingdom of God with one eye than with two eyes to be thrown into **hell**." (Mark 9:47 ESV)

Throughout the Bible, every time the word hell is used, the New World Translation uses the Greek word *Ge·hen′na*.

As most of us know, the term "hell" is usually understood as a place of fiery eternal torment.

Jehovah's Witnesses do not like this translation, so they leave the word "Ge·hen'na" untranslated in their Bible.

There is nothing wrong with leaving a word untranslated. However, there is something definitely wrong when an organization withholds information from their readers in order to influence them into false or incomplete conclusions. What do I mean by this? When an organization leaves a word untranslated, they can take more liberty to give the word a new meaning simply because most readers will not have knowledge of its background. The July 15, 2002 Watchtower is an ideal example of this.

"Gehenna occurs 12 times in the Christian Greek Scriptures, and it refers to the valley of Hinnom, outside the walls of Jerusalem. When Jesus was on earth, this valley was used as a garbage dump, 'where the dead bodies of criminals, and the carcasses of animals, and every other kind of filth was cast.' (Smith's Dictionary of the Bible) The fires were kept burning by adding sulfur to burn up the refuse. Jesus used that valley as a proper symbol of everlasting destruction."[67]

For the most part, we have little reason to reject what the Watchtower is saying here. Personally, I cannot think of a much better illustration for a place of eternal torment than a place for dead, foul things and where the fires never go out.

---

[67] *The Watchtower*, July 15, 2002, page 7

What I do disagree with, is the Watchtower's emphasis on "everlasting destruction" instead of "everlasting torment." They use "Ge·hen′na" as a kind of "proof" that Jesus was referring to instant annihilation. The Watchtower insists no one in early Christianity taught a doctrine of eternal fiery torment. Their publication goes on to ask:

"When did professed Christians adopt the belief in hellfire? Well after the time of Jesus Christ and his apostles. The Apocalypse of Peter (2nd century C.E.) was the first [apocryphal] Christian work to describe the punishment and tortures of sinners in hell."[68]

Friends, I want you to see what is taking place in this writing. It is a prime example of how the

68 *The Watchtower*, July 15, 2002, page 4

Watchtower deceives Jehovah's Witnesses. Reading the above quote, we are left with the following understanding about hellfire?

- Jesus did not teach hellfire
- Jesus's direct disciples did not teach hellfire
- The early church did not teach hellfire

Let's look at these one at a time:

The Watchtower says,
"Jesus did not teach hellfire"

In Luke chapter 16, Jesus tells an intriguing story about a rich man and a poor man. The rich man feasted every day, living lavishly, while ignoring the poor man who desired anything that fell from the rich man's table. Eventually, both men died. The poor man was carried by the angels to Abraham's side and the rich man was buried and went to Hades.

It is here Jesus gets descriptive of the rich man's circumstances. He says,

> "In Hades, being in torment, [the rich man] lifted up his eyes and saw Abraham far off

and Lazarus [the poor man] at his side. And he called out, 'Father Abraham, have mercy on me, and send Lazarus to dip the end of his finger in water and cool my tongue, for I am in anguish in this flame.' But Abraham said, 'Child, remember that you in your lifetime received your good things, and Lazarus in like manner bad things; but now he is comforted here, and you are in anguish. And besides all this, between us and you a great chasm has been fixed, in order that those who would pass from here to you may not be able, and none may cross from there to us.' And he said, 'Then I beg you, father, to send him to my father's house— for I have five brothers—so that he may warn them, lest they also come into this place of torment.'" (Luke 16:23-28 ESV)

Note Jesus's wording: "torment," "have mercy on me," "cool my tongue," "I am in anguish in this flame," and "place of torment."

What does this sound like to you? Instant annihilation or eternal torment in fire? Again, set aside personal feelings and biases. Just be honest with the Scriptures. How can anyone say Jesus did not teach hellfire when here it is?

But if that is not enough, Jesus provided other teaching about eternal torment:

> "Do not fear those who kill the body but cannot kill the soul. Rather fear him who can destroy both soul and body in hell." (Matthew 10:28 ESV)

> "Throw them into the fiery furnace. In that place there will be weeping and gnashing of teeth." (Matthew 13:42 ESV)

> "If your hand causes you to sin, cut it off. It is better for you to enter life crippled than with two hands to go to hell, to the unquenchable fire." (Mark 9:43 ESV)

> "And these will go away into eternal punishment, but the righteous into eternal life." (Matthew 25:46 ESV)

"It is better for you to enter the kingdom of God with one eye than with two eyes to be thrown into hell, where their worm does not die and the fire is not quenched." (Mark 9:47-48)

Again, notice Jesus's words: "fiery furnace," "weeping and gnashing of teeth," "unquenchable fire," "eternal punishment," and "the fire is not quenched."

If we are to read these passages for what they plainly say, this place is obviously much worse than anything we experience in this life. In fact, Jesus said we should fear hell more than what people can do to our bodies. I cannot speak for everyone, but personally, I would rather face instant annihilation than a slow painful death. Taking Jesus's words at face value communicates hell is worse than anything we can imagine.

The Watchtower says,
"The disciples did not teach hellfire"

The Book of Revelation was written by Jesus's beloved disciple, John. Did he teach hellfire?

> "The devil who had deceived them was thrown into the lake of fire and sulfur where the beast and the false prophet were, and they will be tormented day and night forever and ever." (Revelation 20:10 ESV)

Again, look at the wording: "lake of fire," "tormented, day and night forever and ever." Does instant and painless annihilation fit here?

Some may say this is just for the devil, beast, and false prophet, not for humans. However, John's next chapter of Revelation disagrees:

> "As for the cowardly, the faithless, the detestable, as for murderers, the sexually immoral, sorcerers, idolaters, and all liars, their portion will be in the lake that burns with fire and sulfur, which is the second death." (Revelation 21:8 ESV)

These individuals are destined for the same lake of fire the devil, beast, and false prophet are destined for. Can anyone who reads these passages without bias, argue that Jesus's disciple John clearly taught eternal punishment in flames? If so, there is more of this type of narrative from John.

> "If anyone worships the beast and its image and receives a mark on his forehead or on his hand, he also will drink the wine of God's wrath, poured full strength into the cup of his anger, and he will be tormented with fire and sulfur in the presence of the holy angels and in the presence of the Lamb. And the smoke of their torment goes up forever and ever, and they have no rest, day or night, these worshipers of the beast and its image, and whoever receives the mark of its name." (Revelation 14:9-11 ESV)

Again, look at the language here: "God's wrath," "tormented with fire," "the smoke of their torment goes up forever and ever," and "no rest, day or night."

Does annihilation fit? It is obvious from the writings of John, these individuals will be tormented in fire for all eternity. But for those who still prefer to listen to Watchtower indoctrination over the plain teaching of Scripture, perhaps we should look at what John passed down to *his* disciples?

The Watchtower says, "The early church did not teach hellfire"

The Watchtower article claimed the teaching of hellfire came "Well after the time of Jesus Christ and his apostles. The Apocalypse of Peter (2nd century C.E.) was the first [apocryphal] Christian work to describe the punishment and tortures of sinners in hell."

We already listed what Jesus and John taught, but what did the early church have to say about hellfire? To be blunt, the early church taught hellfire right from the beginning! Their earliest documents testifies to a fiery place of eternal punishment.

The Watchtower worded their article to convince readers this doctrine came much later and did not start until an apocryphal text (something of doubtful authenticity).

The Apocalypse of Peter was written between 100-150 AD. This is about 10-60 years after John wrote his Gospel. Most scholars agree this is not a trustworthy source. My questions are:

- Why would the Watchtower use this as a source for hellfire's beginning when it is well known for being untrustworthy?
- Why would they withhold the most credible early church sources on this subject?

The Watchtower mentions some early church fathers like Justin Martyr, Clement of Alexandria, Tertullian, and Cyprian. These men wrote on hellfire between 155 AD – 252 AD. While these are good, I am still left to question, why did they withhold the earliest and most reliable writers?

Ignatius, for example, studied under John the Apostle and succeeded Peter as the Bishop of Antioch. In 110 AD, he wrote,

"Those that corrupt families shall not inherit the kingdom of God. (1 Corinthians 6:9-10) If, then, those who do this as respects the flesh have suffered death, how much more shall this be the case with any one who corrupts by wicked doctrine the faith of God, for which Jesus Christ was crucified! Such an one becoming defiled [in this way], shall go away into everlasting fire."[69]

Those who want to argue this passage will say that the "everlasting fire" mentioned is merely annihilation. But pay special attention to the text. It tells us that the "everlasting fire" is "much more" severe than suffering "death." If annihilation is quick and painless, how can it be so much worse than death?

Another early church document is *The Martyrdom of Polycarp*. This text was written in 155 AD. It provides the martyrdom story and teaching of another disciple of John. Polycarp was the Bishop of Smyrna

---

[69] Ignatius, *The Epistle of Ignatius to the Ephesians*, Chapter 16

and was eventually martyred for his faith. During his sentencing, the Roman Governor threatened,

> "'I'll throw you to the beasts.'
>
> 'Bring on your beasts,' said Polycarp.
>
> 'If you scorn the beasts, I'll have you burned.'
>
> 'You try to frighten me with the fire that burns for an hour, and you forget the fire of hell that never goes out.'"[70]

Here again, Polycarp insinuates that being burned alive for an hour is more pleasant than what the Governor can expect to receive in hell. Does this sound like annihilation?

Polycarp also explained that the martyrs thought lightly of "worldly tortures" because "they kept before their eyes their escape from the eternal and unquenchable fire."[71]

---

[70] Shelley, Bruce L., *Church History in Plain Language*, Nashville: Thomas Nelson Publishers, 1995, page 37

[71] *Martyrdom of Polycarp,* 2:3

So here were have two disciples of John who describes and eternal fire that is much more severe than earthly torcher. To go even further, we can examine the writing of Irenaeus. Irenaeus was the bishop of Lugdunum and a disciple of Polycarp. He was a defender of Christian doctrine and in 189 AD he wrote *Against Heresies*, where he said,

> God "should execute just judgment towards all; that He may send 'spiritual wickednesses,' and the angels who transgressed and became apostates, together with the ungodly, and unrighteous, and wicked, and profane among men, into everlasting fire."[72]

> "The punishment of those who do not believe the Word of God, and despise His advent, and are turned away backwards, is increased; being not merely temporal, but rendered also eternal. For to whomsoever the Lord shall say, 'Depart from me, you

---

[72] Irenaeus, *Against Heresies,* 1:10:10

cursed, into everlasting fire.' (Matthew 25:41) these shall be damned for ever."[73]

Notice Irenaeus said "judgement" will be "eternal fire" and the "punishment" is "increased." This is "not merely temporal" but "eternal." How is this annihilation?

So here we have three church fathers in apostolic succession with Jesus's disciple John. Each of these are more credible than the apocryphal text the Watchtower shared.

One could even go farther with the material found within *Second Clement*. Clement of Rome (not to be confused with Clement of Alexandria) was appointed by Peter and was Bishop of Rome from 88 to 98AD. He was likely the Clement mentioned by Paul in Philippians 4:3. This document was written in 150 A.D. and it discussed the nature of hell several times.

[73] Irenaeus, *Against Heresies*, 4:28:2

"If we neglect his commandments, nothing will rescue us from eternal punishment."[74]

"...those who have sinned and who have denied Jesus by their words or by their deeds are punished with terrible torture in unquenchable fire."[75]

Despite the fact that Jesus, the disciples, and the early church clearly taught an eternal, fiery, punishment that is more severe than earthly torcher, the Watchtower still tries to find ways to contradict all of this material. They attempt to do this by sharing Scriptures like Ecclesiastes 9:5.

"For the living know that they will die, but the dead know nothing, and they have no more reward, for the memory of them is forgotten." (Ecclesiastes 9:5 ESV)

The Watchtower uses this passage to convince their readers that hell cannot be eternal punishment

---

[74] *Second Clement*, 5:5
[75] *Second Clement*, 17:7

because "the dead know nothing." But to interpret it this way, we must assume that if the dead know nothing for hell, then they must know nothing for paradise as well! This goes against any teaching of hell, heaven, or paradise.

The context of this verse gives us a more accurate understanding of what the author of Ecclesiastes is communicating. Looking at the verses before and after verse 5:

> Verses 1-3: Death is the fate of everyone.
>
> Verses 4-6: Death brings everything in life to an end.
>
> Verses 7-10: Make the most of life while you can.

These verses communicate how we are to live while in the land of the living. They are not references to the afterlife. Likewise, the context of the entire book of Ecclesiastes has the same message:

> "Ecclesiastes is written specifically from an earthly perspective. The key phrase,

repeated throughout the book, is 'under the sun,' used about thirty times. [The writer] is commenting on an earth-bound life, 'under the sun,' without God. His conclusion, also repeated throughout the book, is that everything from that perspective is 'vanity.'

When a person dies 'under the sun,' the earthly perspective, without God, is that it's over. He is no longer under the sun. There is no more knowledge to give or be given, just a grave to mark his remains. Those who have died have 'no further reward' in this life; they no longer have the ability to enjoy life like those who are living. Eventually, 'even their name is forgotten'"[76]

---

[76] *What does it mean that the dead know nothing (Ecclesiastes 9:5)?*, Articles on Biblical Topics, https://articles-on-the-bible.schoolpk.org/what-does-it-mean-that-the-dead-know-nothing-ecclesiastes-95/?amp

Said simply, death ends earthly pursuit. The context has nothing to do with eternal reward or punishment.

Another verse the Watchtower uses for their annihilation doctrine is Job 14:13. The same publication goes on to say,

"Consider also the case of the righteous man Job, who suffered much. Wishing to escape his plight, he pleaded: 'Who will grant me this, that thou mayest protect me in hell [Sheol], and hide me till thy wrath pass?'" (Job 14:13, Douay Version)

As is common practice for the Watchtower, they search every Bible translation that has ever been printed in hopes of finding an obscure version that says what they want it to say. Have you ever heard of the Douay Version? Most people haven't. The Watchtower's goal here is to cause people to question the doctrine of hell because if hell is such a bad place, why would Job want to hide there?

Friends, please take the time to research all the Bibles ever printed. You will find that the vast majority either say "Shoel" or "grave." They do not say "hell."

So, what is Shoel? It is not typically a word we use today. Most equate it to the grave. Webster describes it as "the abode of the dead in early Hebrew thought."[77]

I am personally familiar with 55 different Bible translations. When I looked through each of these, I found the Wycliffe Bible to be the only other text that mentions hell in this verse. So, out of 55 Bibles, 2 use the word hell, and that is what the Watchtower uses to convince Jehovah's Witnesses of their doctrine! Do we see a pattern here?

---

[77] *Webster's Dictionary,* https://www.merriam-webster.com/dictionary/Sheol

A Pattern of "Picking and Choosing"

53 Bibles say Job wanted to be protected in "Shoel" or "the grave," while 2 lesser-known Bibles say he wanted protected in "hell." The Watchtower is "picking and Choosing" by:

- Using the translation of a lesser-known Bible.
- Ignoring what the vast majority of more reputable Bibles say.

The context of Ecclesiastes 9:5 refers to life here on earth, not the afterlife. The Watchtower is "picking and Choosing" by:

- Insisting there cannot be eternal torment since the "dead know nothing."
- Ignoring this same principle for "knowing" an eternal reward.

The earliest extra-biblical writings on the doctrine of hell are testimonies from men who learned from

Jesus's apostles. The Watchtower is "picking and Choosing" by:

- Sharing a questionable apocryphal text.
- Ignoring the testimony of the most authoritative church fathers.

Jesus taught: "And these will go away into eternal punishment, but the righteous into eternal life." (Matthew 25:46 ESV) The Watchtower is "picking and Choosing" by:

- Saying the eternal punishment is a temporary annihilation that will not be felt.
- Ignoring this same principle by saying eternal life is eternally enjoyed.

I understand the doctrine of hell is not something we like to dwell on. But we are called to take the Word of God as it is, the pleasant and the not-so-pleasant. Those who are willing to be honest with the text, despite their personal feelings, cannot deny the fact that hell is a major theme in both the Bible and early Christian writings.

PART THREE

WHO IS JESUS?

78 JW.org, Jehovah's Witnesses, *Accept Jehovah's Help to Resist Wicked Spirits,*

Regardless of our personal view of Jesus, few can argue that He has been the subject of more conversation than any human that has ever walked the face of the earth. No one has even come close to His notoriety. This being said, many have conflicting views of this man from Nazareth:

- To Jews, Jesus is a false Messiah.
- To Muslims, Jesus is a mighty prophet.
- To Mormons, Jesus is one of countless gods.
- To Jehovah's Witnesses, Jesus is Michael the Archangel.
- To Christians, Jesus is God in the flesh.

Each of these groups have a defense for what they believe. Likewise, they each have an offense against what the other faiths believe. Since this text focuses on the teaching of the Watchtower, we will only address the two latter faiths.

---

https://www.jw.org/en/library/magazines/watchtower-study-april-2019/gods-help-to-resist-wicked-spirits/

But before we look at Michael through the lenses of Christians and Jehovah's Witnesses, allow me to just ask that we be honest with the Scriptures. That we don't manipulate the Bible or violate scholarly principles. Let us just agree to accept the Bible at face value without trying to force our view upon the text.

Chapter Eight

Is Jesus an Angel
or is He God?

I do not believe anyone will argue that Michael is a mighty warrior who fights valiantly against the enemies of God. Most people have this understanding of Michael, but when it comes to Jehovah's Witnesses, they add the unique belief that Michael and Jesus are the same person. This is unique because one would not typically come to this conclusion from reading the Bible. So, we have to ask, where did this idea come from?

Once again, it is important to note that Jehovah's Witnesses did not always believe this way. Michael the angel joins the long list of subjects in which the Watchtower flip-flopped their beliefs. Early in their doctrine they had a more Biblical understanding of Michael and Jesus.

"Let all the angels of God worship him [that must include Michael, the chief angel, hence Michael is not the Son of God."[79]

Years later, the Watchtower changed their doctrine. *Insight on the Scriptures*, Volume 2 says,

[79] *The Watchtower*, November 11, 1879, page 48

> "Scriptural evidence indicates that the name Michael applied to God's Son before he left heaven to become Jesus Christ."[80]

Time and time again, instead of being a solid rock of doctrinal stability, Watchtower teaching has been "shifting sand" to Jehovah's Witnesses.

So, what evidence does the Watchtower use to support the claim Michael is Jesus? Perhaps it would help if I shared an example from a conversation I had with a Jehovah's Witness. We'll call this Jehovah's Witness "Bob." One day, Bob and I were discussing Jesus and Michael and he shared the following script with me:

Jesus and Michael are a Commander

> *"I promised him that he would become a ruler and commander of many nations." (Isaiah 55:4 ERV)*

> *"At that time Michael, the great commander, will stand up on behalf of the descendants of your people." (Daniel 12:1 GW)*

---

[80] *Insight on the Scriptures*, Volume 2, pages 393

Jesus and Michael are a Keeper of God's People

> _"who will be the keeper of my people Israel."_
> _(Matthew 2:6 BBE)_

> _"At that time shall arise Michael, the great prince who has charge of your people." (Daniel 12:1 ESV)_

Jesus and Michael Appear

> _"When the Lord Jesus appears from heaven."_
> _(2 Thessalonians 1:7 GNB)_

> _"At that time the great angel Michael, who guards your people, will appear." (Daniel 12:1 GNB)_

As you can see, he is explaining how Jesus and Michael share the same titles and attributes. For example, Jesus and Michael are both called "Commanders." Jesus and Michael are both "Keepers of God's People." Jesus and Michael both "Appeared."

If you notice though, out of six different verses, Bob used 5 different translations to make his point. He used the:

1. ERV – Easy-to-Read Version
2. GW - God's Word
3. BBE – Bible in Basic English
4. ESV – English Standard Version
5. GNB – Good News Bible

This is another classic example of Watchtower apologetics. When the wording doesn't fit for one translation, they will scurry through every Bible ever printed (including Bibles no one has ever heard of) until they can find a Bible that says exactly what they want it to say. Friends, this is not scholarship! But to give Bob, and every other Jehovah's Witness the benefit of the doubt, let's pretend all of these passages are 100% legitimate and Jesus and Michael share all of these attributes.

Is it possible there is more than one commander? Could there be more than one person over the centuries who has been the keeper of God's people? Could there be more than one person who has ever appeared? With Watchtower logic, Napoleon and

147

Norman Schwortcolf must be equivalent to Jesus and Michael because they were also commanders.

Moses and David must be equivalent to Jesus and Michael because they were keepers of God's people.

The angel Gabriel and Houdini must be equivalent to Jesus and Michael because they also appeared.

These are obviously ridiculous statements, but I am trying to make a point here. The Watchtower will insist Jesus and Michael are the same because both have been commanders. What they are slow to tell you is that many others have been commanders as well. Likewise many have been a keeper of God's people and many have appeared.

Perhaps it would help if we were a little more specific. Let's look at a few verses that would be unique to *one* person, or at very least, very difficult for anyone else to achieve:

- Jesus is called "mighty God" (Isaiah 9:6). That's a pretty specific title. Who else could possibly be called "mighty God."

  This is interesting! The Bible says Jehovah is called "mighty God" in Deuteronomy 10:17, Jeremiah 32:18, and Isaiah 10:21.[81]

---

[81] When discussing the deity of Christ, Jehovah's Witnesses will often add the rebuttal, "Jesus is not God Almighty. The Bible says Jehovah is almighty, Jesus is just mighty." Their hope is to make a distinction between Jehovah and Jesus by overemphasizing a difference between mighty and almighty.

This is a weak argument because there is nothing in the text that causes the reader to make a distinction between these descriptors. For example, someone could tell you about a fast car on Monday, and on Tuesday tell you about a very fast car. The Watchtower argument insists they must be different cars, but it is very possible the person was talking about the same car both days.

Am I implying the descriptors "mighty" and "almighty" are just a matter of interpretation? No, I am not. There are several Scriptures that identify Jehovah as "mighty God," not "almighty God"… in other words, the same descriptor is used for both Jehovah and Jesus:

- Jesus is called the "first and the last" in Revelation 1:17-18. That's also a specific title. After all, there can only be *one* first and *one* last.

  Wow! Jehovah is also called "the first and the last" in Isaiah 44:6.

- Jesus is called "Alpha and the Omega" in Revelation 22:12-13. That sounds specific to me. Not many people go around calling themselves those names.

  But wait! Jehovah is called "Alpha and the Omega" as well in Revelation 1:8.

- "For your Lord God, speaking of Jehovah, is the God of gods in the Lord of lords, the great, the Mighty." (Deuteronomy 10:17)
- "Return the remnant of Jacob to the mighty God." (Isaiah, 10:21)
- "Oh great and Mighty God." (Jeremiah, 32:18)

Each of these passages are speaking of Jehovah, not Jesus. This clearly shows the Bible does not make a distinction between the terms "mighty" and "almighty," leaving the Jehovah's Witness refuted.

- Let's try a little different perspective. John the Baptist came to prepare the way for Jesus's coming in Mark 1:1-4. I can't imagine he prepared the way for too many people.

  Oh wait! John also prepared the way for Jehovah in Isaiah 40:3.

- Jesus is the "Lord of all" in Acts 10:36. This has to be unique to Jesus because only *One* can be Lord of *all*.

  But wait! Jehovah got us again! He is Lord of all heaven and earth in Matthew 11:25 and Acts 17:24.

The Watchtower tries to rebut these passages by insisting Jesus can be no one other than Michael:

"The Bible states that 'Michael and his angels battled with the dragon . . . and its angels.' (Revelation 12:7) Thus, Michael is the Leader of an army of faithful angels. Revelation also describes Jesus as the Leader of an army of faithful angels.

152

(Revelation 19:14-16) And the apostle Paul specifically mentions "the Lord Jesus" and 'his powerful angels.' (2 Thessalonians 1:7) So the Bible speaks of both Michael and 'his angels' and Jesus and 'his angels.' (Matthew 13:41; 16:27; 24:31; 1 Peter 3:22) Since God's Word nowhere indicates that there are two armies of faithful angels in heaven —one headed by Michael and one headed by Jesus— it is logical to conclude that Michael is none other than Jesus Christ in his heavenly role."[82]

I realize Jehovah's Witnesses are pacifists, so they may need a little help understanding how the military operates. Typically, there are soldiers and officers of different rank within one army. A general can lead the solders that rank lower than him in the one army. A captain can lead the soldiers who rank lower than him in the same army. A sergeant can

[82] Jw.org, *Who is Michael the Archangel?*, 2022, https://www.jw.org/en/library/books/bible-teach/who-is-michael-the-archangel-jesus/

lead the soldiers who rank lower than him in that same army.

The Watchtower is either ignorant of these simple military principles, or they choose to ignore them. They go on to say,

> "It would not make sense for God to set up Jesus and Michael as rival commanders of the holy angels. Rather, it is more reasonable to conclude that both names, Jesus and Michael, refer to the same person."[83]

Think about this for a moment. If it is unacceptable for Jesus and Michael to both lead the angels because only one can lead, then I suppose Jehovah cannot lead His angels because the Jesus/Michael personality is already leading them. After all, according to the Watchtower argument, there can't possibly be more than one person leading! With this kind of thinking, we are forced to conclude that

---

[83] Ibid.

Jesus, Michael, and Jehovah are the same person! Do you see the foolishness here?

The Watchtower will try to rebut another way by saying, "Jesus is Michael because He spoke with the voice of an archangel." They will go on to share 1 Thessalonians 4:16:

> "The Lord himself will descend from heaven with a commanding call, with an archangel's voice and with God's trumpet." (1 Thessalonians 4:16 NWT)

The December 15th 1984 publication of the Watchtower provides their view of this passage:

The Watchtower
Announcing Jehovah's Kingdom

Christmas
Delightful or
Dangerous?

"[Jesus] calls, not with a man's voice as he did then, but with all the power of "an archangel's voice." However, only an archangel can call with an archangel's voice!"[84]

To be clear, the passage says Jesus *came* with the voice of an archangel. It doesn't say Jesus was actually the one speaking. It's very possible an archangel was shouting while Jesus came, just like a trumpet was blowing when Jesus came. But to give the Jehovah's Witnesses the benefit of the doubt and to say Jesus was the one using the archangel's voice, we must ask, why does the Watchtower insist that only an archangel can use an archangel's voice? What criteria do they rely on to make such a claim? Why can God, angels, and demons use a man's voice, but only an angel can use

---

[84] *The Watchtower*, Dec. 15, 1984, page 28

an angel's voice? I am curious how they come to such a conclusion.

To put this into perspective, if I go anywhere and speak, would someone say, "Eric came with a man's voice"? Of course not. That would be a redundant statement. They know I'm a man. They know I'm going to speak with a man's voice. Likewise, if Jesus was indeed an archangel, why would the Bible say He came with an archangel's voice if we know He's an archangel?

Here's how I see this: God created the archangel and God created man. So, if He wanted to use an archangel's voice and a man's voice, he very well could have. There is no reason we should accept the Watchtower's claim that "only an archangel can call with an archangel's voice." There is simply no evidence to support such a claim.

Jesus came with an archangel's voice. This is the same Jesus the Bible repeatedly and emphatically calls God. And if He was indeed the one speaking, it seems likely that since Jesus created the archangel, why could He not speak with the very voice He created?

The 1984 Watchtower publication goes on to say,

> "In fact, he was the archangel, since no other archangel is mentioned in the Bible, nor does the Bible use "archangel" in the plural. "Archangel" means "Chief of the angels." (Thayer's Greek-English Lexicon of the New Testament) Among God's spirit servants, only two names are associated with authority over angels: Michael and Jesus Christ."[85]

The Watchtower publication, *Insight on the Scriptures* reasons down these same lines:

> "Michael is the only one said to be 'the archangel,' meaning 'chief angel,' or 'principal angel.' The term occurs in the Bible in the singular. This seems to imply that there is but one whom God has

---

[85] *The Watchtower*, Dec. 15, 1984, page 28

designated chief, or head, of the angelic host."[86]

Friends, please listen to me. Just because someone uses the word "the" in their title, it does not mean they are the only one. NP Nunez asks us to consider the following:

> Bozo the Clown
> Felix the Cat
> Popeye the Sailor

> According to the Jehovah's Witnesses' logic, Bozo must be the only clown, Felix must be the only cat, and Popeye must be the only sailor, but we know they're not. Those types of names simply tell us what kind of thing someone is, so someone can be called "the something" without being the only "something." And the same holds true for Michael. The fact that he is called "the archangel" could very well mean that he is simply one among several archangels,

---

[86] *Insight on the Scriptures*, Volume 2, pages 393-394

so using the adjective, the, is entirely inconclusive."[87]

When the Watchtower says the Bible does not use "archangel in the plural" I believe they are being purposely manipulative. They know Daniel 10:13 describes Michael as "one of the foremost princes" (Daniel 10:13 NWT)

In other words, Michael is one of several chief princes. This absolutely flies in the face of Watchtower doctrine. They believe Jesus/Michael has a very unique role as the Son of God, but Daniel 10:13 tells us that Michael is "one of the foremost princes." This leads us to believe there may be several archangels, or at very least, other beings with similar authority as Michael. This goes against Watchtower doctrine because they teach that no one else has his power. But again, Daniel says Michael is just "one of." Meanwhile, the Bible tells us Jesus is

---

[87] JP Nunez, *Are Jesus and Michael the Archangel One and the Same?*, Living the Truth the Church Teaches, September 2020, https://catholicstand.com/are-jesus-and-michael-the-archangel-one-and-the-same/

very unique and that He is *not* an angel. Hebrews chapter 1 says:

> "For to which of the angels did God ever say, 'You are my Son?'" (Hebrews 1:5)

This statement implies that God never called an angel "His Son."

> "Let all God's angels worship him." (Hebrews 1:6)

If *all* the angels worship Jesus, this must include Michael, because Michael would be part of "all."

> "He makes his angels winds, and his ministers a flame of fire. But of the Son he says, 'Your throne, O God, is forever and ever.'" (Hebrews 1:7-8)

This clearly implies angels are "winds," but the Son is God Himself.

Friends, this is what I want you to see. Throughout the Watchtower's Michael doctrine, they take bits and pieces of information, and instead of using them in a scholarly way, they find subtle ways to manipulate the material to come up with a totally different message. The Bible never says Jesus is Michael. But the Bible does say Jesus is God and He deserves our heart-felt worship!

Chapter Nine

Early Church Testimony

325 A.D. That's when it all started. Before then, every Christian knew the truth. Jehovah was God and Jesus was His son. No one questioned these things until the Council of Nicaea came along and changed everything.

[88]The Roman Emperor Constantine was desperate for unity between the Christian Church and the Roman state. So, at the Council of Nicaea, he strong-armed the Christian bishops,

---

[88] *Carved from Stone,* https://statues-and-monuments.tumblr.com/post/60209844633/statues-and-monuments-emperor-constantine-by/amp

forcing them to embrace pagan ways in order to make the teachings of Jesus more palatable to Rome. One of these pagan teachings was Jesus is God.

This is church history according to the Watchtower. They teach that before 325 A.D. and the Council of Nicaea, no one would have imaged the idea "Jesus is God." In fact, if anyone would have presented such an idea to the early church fathers, they would have scoffed at it. But then we read the New Testament!

[89]Perhaps Thomas wasn't told these details when he called Jesus, "My Lord and my God."

---

[89] *Faith and Reason*, http://faithandreasonblog.blogspot.com/p/about-this-blog.html

[90]Maybe Matthew did not get the memo when he called Jesus, "God with us."

[91]Maybe John was just joking when he said, "the Word was God."

---

[90] *Reading   and   Art*,
readingandart.blogspot.com/2013/11/frans-hals.html
[91] In search of the Apostles, *John "The Beloved'*,
https://discover.hubpages.com/religion-philosophy/In-search-of-the-Apostles-John-The-Beloved-part-2

[92]Perhaps someone should have punished Paul for calling Jesus, "God and Savior."

[93]Maybe Jesus Himself needed a Jehovah's Witness to remind Him not to repeatedly apply divine Scripture to Himself or to allow people to worship Him.

Not surprisingly, the Watchtower has excuses for these Bible passages. After all, they have been honing their doctrine for at least 150 years now. In

---

[92] *The Life of the Apostle Paul*, https://reasonabletheology.org/life-of-paul/

[93] *How Did Jehovah's Witnesses Get Their Name?*, JW.org, https://www.jw.org/en/jehovahs-witnesses/faq/name-jehovahs-witnesses/

that time, they have taken all their easy to see deceptions and masked over them. However, 150 years of modifying their religion still wasn't enough time because the evidence for Jesus's deity is too overwhelming. You just can't hide it all! Not only are there at a plethora of Scriptures that point to Jesus's deity, but there are also multiple early church father quotes, all before 325 A.D. that say, "Jesus is God." Some of these men learned directly from Jesus Apostles.

[94]Polycarp was a disciple of John. He lived between 69 A.D. – 155 A.D. (170 years before the Council of Nicaea). He said,

"… to all those under heaven who will yet believe in **our Lord and God**

---

[94]   The   Westminister   Standard,   *Polycarp*, https://thewestminsterstandard.org/polycarp-2/

Jesus Christ and in his Father who raised him from the dead."[95]

[96]Ignatius was another man who studied under John. He lived between 50 A.D. – 140 A.D. (185 years before the council of Nicaea). He said,

"For **our God, Jesus the Christ**, was conceived by Mary according to God's plan."[97]

[95] Polycarp, Letter to the Philippians
[96] Ignatius Loyola, https://snl.no/Ignatius_Loyola
[97] Ignatius, Letter to the Ephesians

 [98]A church apologist named Justin Martyr lived between 100 A.D. – 165 A.D. (160 years before the Council of Nicaea). He said,

"The Father of the universe has a Son; who also, being the first-begotten Word of God, **is even God**. And of old **He appeared in the shape of fire and in the likeness of an angel to Moses** and to the other prophets; but now in the times of your reign, having, as we before said, become Man by a virgin..."[99]

---

[98] *Early Church Fathers: Justin Martyr*, https://www.redeemersarasota.org/early-church-fathers-justin-martyr/

[99] Justin Martyr, *First Apology*, 63. ANF, I:184

[100]Tertullian was an early church author who lived between 160 A.D. - 225 A.D. (100 years before the Council of Nicaea). He said,

"For God alone is without sin; and the only man without sin is Christ, since **Christ is also God**."[101]

An early church theologian named Origen lived between 185 A.D. - 254 A.D. (71 years before the Council of Nicaea). He was the first to put together the 27 New

---

[100] Tertullian: *God Creates in (by) Wisdom*, http://www.readreflectwrite.com/2020/09/tertullian-god-creates-in-by-wisdom.html

[101] Tertullian, *Treatise on the Soul*, page 41

Testament books as we know it today. He said,

[102] "And as no one ought to be offended, seeing God is the Father, that **the Savior is also God**; so also, since the Father is called omnipotent, no one ought to be offended that the Son of God is also called omnipotent."[103]

As we can see, not only are there multiple Bible passages that say, "Jesus is God," but there are also multiple early church fathers (all before 325 A.D.) that said, "Jesus is God." This absolutely contradicts Watchtower teaching.

At this point, it is only fitting to see what the Council of Nicaea was really about in 325 A.D.

---

[102] *A History of Orthodoxy vs. Heresy*, Part III: Philo, Clement and Origen, https://fireofnorea.com/2015/06/13/a-history-of-orthodoxy-vs-heresy-part-iii-philo-clement-and-origen/
[103] Origen, *De Principiis*, Book 1, Chapter 2, Section 10

[104]Back then, there was a troublemaker in the church who was teaching strange doctrines. This man's name was Arius, and one of his doctrines was the idea that Jesus was not God.

Arius would often use bizarre reasoning to try and prove his points. When the church decided to deal with this, they assembled the Council of Nicaea, consisting of at least 250 bishops. After a time of deliberation, 2 bishops sided with Arius while everyone else called his teaching heresy. This led to his banishment.

From there, Arianism was sporadic. It would occasionally pop up here and there throughout

[104] *The Escape of Athanasius,* 356, https://landmarkevents.org/history-highlights-week-of-february-5/

history but for the most part, it was uncommon. However, after 15 centuries of lying dormant, a man named Charles Taze Russell came along and resurrected it. As we know, Arianism is the Watchtower today.

If I can leave you with anything, test and approve of what you hear. If there is layer upon layer, generation upon generation of evidence, all confounding what you are being told, reject what you are being told! The Bible and church history make up a great crowd of witnesses that testify to the deity of Christ. The Watchtower tries very hard to pervert these teachings. Thankfully their doctrine was rejected back in 325 A.D. It is only fitting we do the same thing today.

PART FOUR

THE MULTI-HEADED GOD OF THE JEHOVAH'S WITNESSES

If you go on Jehovah's Witness websites, you will find the Watchtower describes the Trinity as a pagan belief and will often accompany this teaching with one of the following pictures. Their agenda is to convince you that this is the Trinity and at some point in time, Christians worshipped such a god.[105] [106] [107]

---

[105] JW.org, Jehovah's Witnesses, *Myth 4: God is a Trinity*, https://www.jw.org/en/library/magazines/wp20091101/myth-god-is-a-trinity/

[106] JW.org, Jehovah's Witnesses, *Should You Believe in the Trinity?*, https://www.jw.org/en/library/magazines/g201308/trinity/

[107] JW.org, Jehovah's Witnesses, *Is God a Trinity?*, https://www.jw.org/en/bible-teachings/questions/trinity/

The reality is, there isn't a residue of evidence that says the Christian Church worshiped such images. The Trinity is not the belief of three gods. It is a monotheistic belief. Trinitarians worship the same God the Jews worshiped in the Old Testament and the early church worshiped in the New Testament.

Jehovah's Witnesses will try to defend these Watchtower claims, but all you have to do is ask them to provide historical evidence that backs up their accusations. They can't because these are images of pagan gods who had nothing to do with orthodox Christianity. It's a subtle deceptive trick designed to make people question sound Biblical teaching.

Why do Christians adhere to the Trinity doctrine? Because the Bible gives us no other choice. It has a consistent message of one God who saves the souls of man. This one God has revealed Himself many times as three distinct persons... the Father, the Son, and the Holy Spirit. The Watchtower tries to discredit the Bible's message here. But the reality is we cannot adhere to the Bible and reject the Trinity at the same time. Those who do, find themselves on shifting sand.

Christians do not follow some strange three-headed Egyptian or Babylonian god. They follow Jesus Christ because He is the Way, the Truth, and the Life. He is the solid rock on which we stand. This is what the Bible teaches.

Jehovah's Witnesses, on the other hand, find themselves forced to follow the leaders of the Watchtower, even though they have a 150-year history of shifting sand, changing core doctrines.

The sad reality is the governing body is the god of Jehovah's Witnesses because the Watchtower's structure is set up in such a way that Jehovah's Witnesses must follow the governing body even when it sways from the Word of God.

Let's face it, if the Watchtower decides to make up another heretically unbiblical amendment to their doctrine, millions of Jehovah's Witnesses will blindly follow along without question, simply because the Watchtower says so.

Friends, don't be that person. Put your trust in the God of Heaven, not a group of men who pervert His Word. Read the Bible for what it plainly says.

Chapter Ten

Jehovah's Witnesses Expose Heresy

Have you ever tried talking to a Jehovah's Witness about the Deity of Christ, when the Jehovah's Witness cuts you off,

> *If Jesus is God, why did he pray to Jehovah in the Garden of Gethsemane? Was he praying to himself?*

That seems like a fair question. After all, does God pray to God? So you attempt to answer, but before you can explain what is happening in this passage, the Jehovah's Witness cuts you off again with another question.

> *If Jesus is God, why did Jesus say in Matthew 24:36, "No one knows when the end will come, not even the Son, only the Father"?*

This is mildly frustrating because you would like to first explain why Jesus was praying, but the Jehovah's Witness doesn't give you the chance to…

> *If Jesus is God, why did he say in John 14:28, "My father is greater than I"?*

Now you're just getting annoyed because you aren't even given the decency to finish your thou…

> *If Jesus is God, why does 1 Corinthians 11:3 say Jehovah is the head of Christ?*

Frustration becomes annoyance and annoyance becomes ange…

> *If Jesus is God, why does 1 Corinthians 15 say he will be made subject to God?*

Jehovah's Witnesses love to share these passages. Before you try to address the first scripture, many will cut you off with the next, and the next, and the next. They do this in hopes of overwhelming you with so many passages that you cannot possibly answer them.

It's times like these that you may be tempted to put aside your walk with the Lord for a few satisfying moments. But don't do it! The zealous Jehovah's Witness may not realize it, but he is actually fighting for orthodox Trinitarianism! They think they are "destroying" Christian theology, but in reality, they are helping us with an age-old heresy.

You may be asking, how is he defending the Trinity when it seems pretty obvious he is trying to discredit it?

When a Jehovah's Witness asks,

> *"If Jesus is God, why did he pray? Why didn't he know the time of the end? Why is the Father greater? Why is God his head? Why is he subject to God?"*

When they ask these things, they are trying to force Christianity into an age-old heresy called modalism. Modalism is the belief that God is only one person, not three. And this one person reveals himself in three different forms or modes. In other words, one minute God will take on the form of the Father. The next he may take on the form of the Son. And the next he may take on the form of the Holy Spirit. One person showing up in three ways. This is not orthodox Trinitarianism and we should join the Jehovah's Witnesses in condemning such beliefs.

The Trinity doctrine, on the other hand, is one God who eternally exists in three persons. Moses said in Deuteronomy 6:4, "Hear O Israel: the Lord our God, the Lord is one." The Father is called God in 2 Peter 1:17. The Bible also tells us Jesus is called God in John 20:28. At the same time, Jesus spoke to God as His Father, emphasizing He is a different person than God the Father.

Fifty days after Jesus' resurrection, the Holy Spirit came upon the early church in a powerful way. The Bible calls the Holy Spirit God in Acts 5:1-9. But He is not the same person as the Father or the Son.

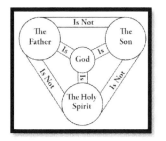

The Trinity then, helps us speak correctly about God. The Bible tells us the Father is called God. The Bible tells us the Son is called God. And the Bible tells us the Holy Spirit is called God. At the same time, the Son is not the Father, the Father is not the Holy Spirit, and the Holy Spirit is not the Son. One God, three persons.

This is revealed in Jesus's baptism:

1. Jesus was coming out of the river.
2. The Father was in heaven saying, "This is my beloved Son in whom I am well please."
3. The Spirit was descending in the form of a dove.

Three different persons, in three different places, doing three different things. One God, three persons.

When we view God as one person who takes on different modes, it does not make sense how they can all be present at one time at Jesus' baptism. And it makes no sense why Jesus prayed, or why He didn't know the time of the end, or why the Father is greater, or why God is Christ's head, or why He is subject to the Father. However, if God is one eternal being existing in three persons, then all of this makes perfect sense. Philippians 2 fills in many of the details,

> "Christ Jesus, who, though he was in the form of God, did not count equality with God a thing to be grasped, but emptied himself, by taking the form of a servant, being born in the likeness of men. And being found in human form, he humbled himself by becoming obedient to the point of death, even death on a cross." (Philippian's 2:5-8 ESV)

Consider this passage friends. Christ was in the form of God, but he emptied Himself of His deity and came to earth in the form of a servant. He became our perfect example as one obedient to the Father: praying to the Father, joining the Father in His work, depending on the Father, etc. Several passages support this,

- "for a little while [Jesus] was made lower than the angels." (Hebrews 2:9 ESV)
- "In the beginning was the Word, and the Word was with God, and the Word was God... And the Word became flesh and dwelt among us, and we have seen his glory, glory as of the only Son from the Father." (John 1:1, 14 ESV)
- Jesus said, "And now, Father, glorify me in your own presence with the glory that I had with you before the world existed." (John 17:5 ESV)

Some may argue,

> *"How can Jesus be God if He was inferior to His Father?"*

These individuals confuse inferiority with subjection. The Bible never tells us Jesus was inferior to His Father. It says He was subject to His Father. This refers to the roles of the Father and the Son.

Think of it this way, if I am an obedient son, I will subject myself to my father. I will not necessarily think I am inferior to my father, but I will always honor my dad and see his role as "greater" than my own. This ties into 1 Corinthians 11:3 where it says, "the head of every man is Christ, the head of a wife is her husband, and the head of Christ is God." (1 Corinthians 11:3 ESV)

The Bible teaches us that the man is the "head" of the household. Does this mean wives are inferior to their husbands? Absolutely not. They simply play different roles. Likewise, the Son of God has a different role than the Father. And the Holy Spirit has a different role than both the Son and the Father. None are inferior to the other. The same principle is shown in 1 Corinthians 15:24-28 where Jesus is subject to His Father. Jesus has the role of an obedient son, so He subjects Himself to His Father.

So, how do we answer Jehovah's Witnesses' toughest questions? All of them can be answered quite simply with one answer!

Why did Jesus pray?

Because He emptied Himself to become a servant to the Father!

Why didn't Jesus know the time of the end?

Because He emptied Himself to become a servant to the Father!

Why did Jesus say, "the Father is greater?"

Because He emptied Himself to become a servant to the Father!

Why does the Bible say the Father is the head of Christ?

Because He emptied Himself to become a servant to the Father!

Why does the Bible say Christ will be subject to the Father?

Because He emptied Himself to become a servant to the Father!

This seems simple enough, but to those who need more explanation, consider something: If two humans have a child, their offspring is human. And hypothetically, if there were two deities, and they had a child, their offspring would be deity. But if a deity and a human had a child, that child would be both human and deity.

When God caused the virgin to be with child, Mary had to carry Jesus in her womb for nine months. After this time was complete, she gave birth to a human baby. She had to nurse Him. She had to cloth Him. She had to provide shelter for Him. And when Jesus became a man, the Bible says He still became hungry, thirsty, and weak. All these aspects reveal that Jesus was fully human. And as a human, He did not know everything. He had to grow in knowledge. He had to be dependent upon His Father. He had to pray to His Father and be subject to His Father. Just like the Bible says.

At the same time, Jesus obviously did things that went beyond human capabilities. Humans cannot open the eyes of a blind man by putting mud on them. Humans cannot put their fingers in a deaf man's ear and cause him to hear. Humans cannot cause a fig tree to wither by speaking to it. Humans cannot tell a dead man to come back to life after being in grave four days. And humans cannot raise themselves from a torturous death. Jesus could do these things because He is not just human, He is also deity!

He voluntarily made Himself a human servant while remaining God. And while He was on earth, He watched where His Father was working and then joined Him in His work.

So, yes, Jesus prayed and subjected Himself to His Father. Thank you Jehovah's Witnesses for pointing that out. And yes, it makes no sense for Jesus to be the same person as the Father and pray to Himself or subject Himself to Himself. Thank you Jehovah's Witnesses for pointing that out.

So instead of getting mad at our Jehovah's Witness friends, we really should be thanking them. I am grateful that instead of disagreeing with each other all the time, Christians and Jehovah's Witnesses can join forces against the heresy of Modalism.

Chapter Eleven

The Worst Excuse for Rejecting the Trinity

Of all the foolish reasons to rejecting something, the worst one has got to be:

> *"The Trinity cannot be true because the word Trinity is not found in the Bible."*

It's true, the word "Trinity" is not mentioned in the Bible. But neither is the word "omniscient." Does this mean God is not all knowing? Of course not. The doctrine of God's omniscience is very much present in the Bible. Likewise, the Bible does not use the word "Trinity" but the doctrine is throughout the Bible's pages.

We already saw the Trinity in Jesus's baptism. The same can be seen in the Great Commission:

"Go therefore and make disciples of all nations, baptizing them in the name of the Father and of the Son and of the Holy Spirit," (Matthew 28:19 ESV)

Here we have the Father, Son, and the Spirit but notice the "name" is singular. How can the name be singular if the Bible tells us the Father is called God, the Son is called God, and the Holy Spirit is called God? This is explained by the Trinity. Three separate persons who make up one God.

"I am the first, and I am the last; and beside me there is no God." (Isaiah 44:6)

We find the Trinity in other areas of Scriptures as well:

- "Then God said, 'Let **us** make man in **our** image.'" (Genesis 1:26)
- "Let **us** go down and confound their language." (Genesis 11:7)
- Isaiah said, "I heard the voice of the Lord saying, 'Whom shall I send, and who will go for **us**?'" (Isaiah 6:8)

Why is God describing Himself in the plural when the Bible plainly says there is only one God?

> "Hear, O Israel: The Lord our God, the Lord is one." (Deuteronomy 6:4)

This is easily explained through the Trinity. One God who is a plural of persons. The Bible has much more to say about this:

> "In the beginning was the Word, and the Word was with God, and the Word was God." (John 1:1 ESV)

Again, when Jehovah's Witnesses hear this passage, they immediately get on edge. They say, "No, no, no, it should not read 'the Word was God.' it should read 'the Word was a god.'"

For them, they are taught that Jesus is a lesser god, created by Jehovah. Just for today, let's ignore what Greek scholars say and entertain this Watchtower reinterpretation. What would happen to the Bible's message if Jesus is "a god" that was created by Jehovah? We immediately find a problem in Isaiah 43:

"I am he. Before me no god was formed, nor shall there be any after me. I, I am the Lord, and besides me there is no savior." (Isaiah 43:10-11 ESV)

Friends, if I am a Jehovah's Witness at this point, I am beside myself. I am screaming out to the Watchtower, saying, "Please explain these things to me!" How can Jesus be a created, lesser god when this passage plainly tells us there is no other god formed after me? And how can there be no savior beside me when Jesus and the Father are both called savior? How can there be two saviors?

This does not make sense to a Jehovah's Witness. They have to rely on the most bizarre, far-fetched, heretical, Arian indoctrination to make this work, and it still doesn't work!

But if I'm a Trinitarian, I'm sitting back, calm, cool, and collective. I don't have to make up excuses for why Jesus is called God. I don't have to make up excuses why the Holy Spirit is called God. I don't have to make up excuses for why God describes himself in the plural. I don't have to make up excuses why the Bible says there is only one God and besides Him there are no others formed. I don't have to make us excuses why the Bible says there should only be one savior.

All of these things make perfect sense to me because it's what the Bible teaches. I don't have to come up with far-fetched, bizarre scenarios to make the Bible say what I want it to say. I can read the Bible for what it plainly says. The Bible teaches that the Father, Son, and Holy Spirit are distinct persons with different functions, and they are all identified as God. This is Trinity.

Friends, don't allow some organization to force a heretical doctrine upon you. Read the Bible for what it plainly says. If you do that and reject heresy, the pieces will fit together just fine.

Chapter 12

Trinity in the Resurrection

Have you ever seen the research presented by Flat-Earth Theorists? These individuals teach that instead of being a sphere, the earth is a flat disc floating through space. Their research sounds convincing at first, until you compare it with the mountains of evidence that proves the Earth is spherical.

Likewise, there are those who believe that the holocaust never happened. These individuals claim the holocaust was a hoax made up by Jews so they could win sympathy to regain their homeland. This also sound convincing until you compare their research with the mountain the evidence proving the holocaust took place.

Then we come to the Watchtower. I have had my fair share of conversations with Jehovah's Witnesses, who asked me,

"If Jesus is God, then who raised Him from the Dead?"

They ask this because the Watchtower teaches them Jesus did not raise Himself, but was raised by Jehovah. However, what they fail to receive is the Bible plainly and clearly teaches Jesus raised himself, and that His resurrection absolutely points to the Trinity.

For starters, we can agree with the Watchtower when they say, "Jehovah raised Jesus." The book of Acts says,

> "and you killed the Author of life, whom God raised from the dead." (Acts 3:15 ESV)

What they hesitate to tell you is the Bible also teaches the Spirit raised Jesus from the dead. The book of Romans says,

> "If the Spirit of him who raised Jesus from the dead dwells in you, he who raised Christ Jesus from the dead will also give

life to your mortal bodies through his Spirit who dwells in you." (Romans 8:11 ESV)

But what they *really* don't want you to hear is that the Bible plainly teaches Jesus raised himself. The gospel of John says,

"Jesus answered them, 'Destroy this temple, and in three days I will raise it up...' But he was speaking about the temple of his body." (John 2:19,21 ESV)

Let's read that again, "Destroy this temple and in three days I will raise it up."

One more time, "I will raise it up."

Please feel free to put this book down. Take the time to thoroughly research the context of these verses. Look at the chapters before, look at the chapters after. Whatever you have to do to exhaust all excuses and find the true explanation for these verses. At the end of the day, you will find out that Jesus is saying He will raise himself.

If indeed you are a Jehovah's Witness who had a lifetime of Watchtower indoctrination, you are probably struggling about now. I understand that. Better yet, Jesus understands that. That's why He provided more evidence for you from His Word!

> "For this reason the Father loves me, because I lay down my life that I may take it up again. No one takes it from me, but I lay it down of my own accord. I have authority to lay it down, and I have authority to take it up again. This charge I have received from my Father." (John 10:17,18 ESV)

Read that again, "I have authority to take it up again. This charge I have received from my Father."

One more time, "I have authority to take it up again."

Again, put this book down. Look at the chapters before and the chapters after. Whatever you have to do the exhaust any questions you may have. At the end of the day, you will find the context is plainly saying, Jesus will raise himself.

So, the Bible plainly says the Father will raise Jesus. The Spirit will raise Jesus. And Jesus will raise Jesus. The Bible also says, "God raised Jesus." Does this not sound like the Trinity doctrine?

Before we get too far ahead of ourselves, maybe we'd better first see what the Watchtower has to say about these verses! After all, we can't *possibly* know the truth without finding out what they teach! We already checked these verses in their context. The Watchtower will *surely* explain all of this without trying to add any strange or bizarre excuses!

A 1973 Watchtower publication shares the passage from John chapter 2, "Break down this temple and in three days I will raise it up." They also share John chapter 10, "I have the right to receive it back again." They also share

Romans 8:11, "the spirit of him who raised up Jesus from the dead."[108]

Ironically, the Watchtower lists all the above verses that point to the Trinity. And what do they conclude after seeing all these verses? Their conclusion:

> "Jesus Christ simply could not have meant that he would raise himself up from the dead."[109]

What! After seeing all these plain and clear verses, how could they come to such a conclusion?

In John 10:17, 18, the Watchtower used a translation that reads, "I have the right to **receive** it back again." (New English Bible.)

Again, I took the time to look up every Bible I could possibly think of (55 different Bibles). These are all the standard Bibles most people use: the King James, NIV, ESV, NASB, etc. Of every one of those 55 Bibles, I found 52 that say, "Jesus will **take**

---

[108] *The Watchtower*, June 1, 1973, page 350
[109] *The Watchtower*, June 1, 1973, page 351

back." This insinuates He has the power and authority to take back His life. This is different from "receive back."

I must point out that "receive your life back" does not disagree with Jesus raising himself. It merely takes away much of the force the "take back" message has. The three translations that say "receive back" were the:

- CEV: Contemporary English version
- TS2009: The Scripture 2009 Version
- NEB: The New English Bible

As mentioned several times before, whenever the Watchtower runs into a passage that gives them trouble or contradicts her doctrine, they search for any Bible they can find that has different wording, anything they can use outside of the standard translation of the passage. Friends, this is not scholarship! To overlook all the Bibles in favor of translations that frankly no one has ever heard of is not scholarship.

I shared this chapter for three reasons:

1. The Bible plainly tells us Jesus raised himself.

2. The Bible tells us the Father raised Jesus, the Holy Spirit raised Jesus, and Jesus raised Jesus. This absolutely points to the Trinity.

3. The final reason I share this is because when we read these Watchtower pages without researching anything else, they sound convincing.

Half of the time they use wordy language that is hard to follow or they use obscure Bible translations that support their stance. They put the words together in such a way that it causes readers to believe something contrary to what the Bible plainly says. This is why I continually emphasize, read the Bible for what it plainly says. Do not let someone else manipulate you!

Reading the Bible Without the Watchtower Leads to Christianity

Over the last few years of studying Watchtower literature, I have come across remarkable statements. I have read some catastrophic contradictions, some mind-blowing manipulations, I've read some preposterous prophecies, disturbing doctrines, and some terrible twisting of Scripture. But of all of these deceptive techniques, it's probably when the Watchtower tells the truth that I find their words the most surprising.

What do I mean by this? Looking at the Watchtower's founder, Charles Taze Russell, he said something unexpected in a September 15, 1910 publication:

"Not only do we find that people cannot see the divine plan in studying the Bible by itself, but we see, also, that if anyone lays the Scripture Studies aside, even after he has used them, after he has become familiar with them, after he has read them for ten years—if he then lays them aside and ignores them and goes to the Bible alone, though he has understood his Bible for ten years, our experience shows that within two years he goes into darkness."[110]

Friends, this is a remarkable statement! Charles Taze Russell is saying it doesn't matter if you have been a Jehovah's Witness for ten years. You can be seasoned in Watchtower doctrine. You can know it forward and backwards. If you step away from it and read nothing but the Bible, in two years' time,

---

regardless of how seasoned you are, you will step away from what the Watchtower teaches.

In other words, reading the Bible without Watchtower doctrine, takes you away from Watchtower doctrine! That's incredible! Think about that for a moment. Reading the Bible by itself brings you to different conclusions than the Watchtower teaches.

Russell did not want Jehovah's Witnesses to read the Bible without his "help." So, over the years, the Watchtower added some extra teachings to remind Jehovah's Witnesses how much they "need" their organization. The Watchtower July 1 1965 says,

Jehovah "does not impart his holy spirit and an understanding and appreciation of his Word apart from his visible organization." [111]

---

[111] *The Watchtower*, July 1 1965, page 391

"The Bible is an organizational book and belongs to the Christian congregation as an organization, not to individuals, regardless of how sincerely they may believe that they can interpret the Bible. For this reason the Bible cannot be properly understood without Jehovah's visible organization in mind."[112]

These are interesting claims, especially from a group of people who insist they are best Bible students. In reality, these Watchtower quotes are strategically written to help them maintain control of Jehovah's Witnesses. It is a way of saying, "Don't even try to read the Bible without our influence. You need us to understand the Bible."

But this is just the tip of the iceberg. As we dig deeper in Watchtower material, we learn what they

---

[112] *The Watchtower*, Oct. 1 1967, page 587

fear the most. The Watchtower, August 15, 1981 says,

"They try to sow doubts and to separate unsuspecting ones from the bounteous "table" of spiritual food spread at the Kingdom Halls of Jehovah's Witnesses, where truly there is 'nothing lacking.' They say that it is sufficient to read the Bible exclusively, either alone or in small groups at home. But, strangely, through such 'Bible reading,' they have reverted right back to the apostate doctrines that commentaries by Christendom's clergy were teaching 100 years ago…"[113]

---

[113] *The Watchtower*, August 15, 1981, pages 28-29

This is an amazing admission! The Watchtower openly states that if Jehovah's Witnesses step away from the Watchtower's doctrine and read nothing but the Bible, they will likely reject their doctrine and cling to Christianity.

So… reading the Bible by itself without the Watchtower's help causes people to reject the Watchtower? Reading the Bible by itself without the Watchtower's help causes people to embrace Christianity?

Friends, over the years of talking to Jehovah's Witnesses, I have learned to resist the temptation of calling the Watchtower a cult. I do this because it's rarely effective. When we call the Watchtower a cult, at that point the Jehovah's Witnesses' brain shuts down. They get a glazed look in their eye, and then reject everything else you have to say.

But after looking at all of this information, I just can't help myself. If you are in a religion, an organization, a faith, or a doctrine that tells you what the Bible says and then tells you not to read the

Bible without them telling you what it says, you are probably in a cult!

We see the same thing with the Mormons and the Muslims. If a Mormon decides to read nothing but the Bible without the "help" of the *Book of Mormon*, *Doctrine and Covenants*, or *Pearl of Great Price*, in a matter of time, he or she is going to step away from Joseph Smith doctrine and is going to embrace the truth. If a Muslim decides to read nothing but the Bible without the "help" of the Qur'an, the Hadith, or any of the other nonsense Muhammad said, in a matter of time, he or she is going to step away from Islam and will embrace the truth.

Please listen, I really want you to take a moment to think about where you are in life. If you find yourself following an organization that demands 100% allegiance, while at the same time, has a history of contradiction and inconsistency, you are probably in a cult.

The Good News is, there is a way out! His name is Jesus! He is asking you to stop drinking the poison and start reading His Word for what it plainly says.

If the Bible says Jesus is God and He created all things, then accept that. If the Bible says Jesus should be worshipped and He is the only way to salvation, then receive that. You'll be so glad you did!

I hope this book blessed you and helps you in your pursuit of Truth.

SO MANY EXCUSES FOR SO MANY PASSAGES

There are two ways to approach the Bible. We can read it for what it plainly says or we can read it for what we want it to say. The first of these approaches will require us to empty ourselves of our agendas, preconceived ideas, and from time to time, our comfort. It will require that we get ourselves out of the way and just allow God to speak.

The second of these approaches will allow us to keep our agendas, preconceived ideas, and our comfort. We can make the Bible say whatever seems right in our own eyes. All we have to do is ignore a few passages here and make a few excuses there.

With a little creativity, we can force the Bible to fit our worldview.

But my question is: Why not read the Bible for what it plainly says? Why adhere to a belief system that has to make so many excuses for so many Scriptures? We only have one chance to live faithfully for God. Why allow someone else to manipulate you? Especially when there have been so many other false religions doing the same thing?

- Islam forces the Bible to say Muhammad is the Promised Helper. Muslims will argue this point to the bitter end, even though a conservative reading of the Bible proves the Holy Spirit is the Promised Helper.

- The Church of Jesus Christ of Latter-Day Saints forces the Bible to say we can become gods. Mormons will argue this point to the bitter end, even though a conservative reading of the Bible proves there is only one God and besides Him, there is no other.

- The Progressive Church forces the Bible to say God approves of the homosexual lifestyle. LGBTQ people will argue this point to the bitter end, even though a conservative reading of the Bible proves homosexuality is an abomination in God's sight.

- The Watchtower forces the Bible to say Jesus is Michael the Archangel. Jehovah's Witnesses will argue this point to the bitter end, even though a conservative reading of the Bible proves Jesus is God.

Examine the immense amount of material that all says the same thing:

Jesus is Called:

- "mighty God" (Isaiah 9:6)
- "God with us" (Matthew 1:23)
- "God" (John 1:1)
- "only begotten God" (John 1:18)
- "my Lord and my God" (John 20:28)
- "great God and Savior" (Titus 2:13)

- "God" (Hebrews 1:8)
- "God and Savior" (2 Peter 1:1)

Jesus Received Worship Multiple Times:

- "…come to worship him." (Matthew 2:2)
- "…come and worship him." (Matthew 2:8)
- "…they fell down and worshiped him." (Matthew 2:11)
- "…those in the boat worshiped him" (Matthew 14:33)
- "…took hold of his feet and worshiped him." (Matthew 28:9)
- "…they worshiped him." (Matthew 28:17)
- "…they worshiped" (Luke 24:52)
- "… he worshiped him." (John 9:38)
- "… angels worship him." (Hebrews 1:6)

Jesus Did Things Only God Should Do:

- Jesus forgives sins (Mark 2:5-7)

- Jesus is the only name by which to be saved (Acts 4:12)
- Jesus's name is above every name (Philippians 2:9)
- Jesus created all things (Colossians 1:16)

The Early Church called Jesus:

- "our Lord and God" (Polycarp 69 - 155 A.D
- "our God" (Ignatius 50 - 140? A.D.)
- "God" (Justin Martyr 100 - 165 A.D.)
- "God" (Tertullian 160 - 225 A.D.)
- "God" (Origen (185 - 254 A.D.)

Jesus and Jehovah Share Attributes:

- Jehovah knows all things. (1 John 3:20) Jesus knows all things. (John 16:30)
- Jehovah is the only one who knows the hearts of all men. (1 Kings 8:39) Jesus knows the hearts of all men. (John 2:24-25)

- Jehovah is our healer. (Exodus 15:26) Jesus heals us. (Acts 9:34)
- Jehovah God dwells in us. (2 Corinthians 6:16) Jesus is in us. (Romans 8:10)
- Jehovah is the giver of life who will not allow His people to be snatched out of His hand. (Deuteronomy 32:39) Jesus is the giver of life who will not allow His people to be snatched out of His hand. (John 10:28)
- Jehovah is present everywhere. (Proverbs 15:3) Jesus is omnipresent. (Matthew 28:20)
- Jehovah's nature does not change. (Malachi 3:6) Jesus' nature does not change. (Hebrews 13:8).
- Jehovah's glory is not to be given to another. (Isaiah 42:8) Jesus shares Jehovah's glory. (John 17:5)
- Jehovah is the mighty God. (Isaiah 10:21) Jesus is the mighty God (Isaiah 9:6)

- Jehovah is the first and the last. (Isaiah 44:6) Jesus is the first and the last. (Revelation 1:17-18)
- Jehovah is the Alpha and the Omega. (Revelation 1:8) Jesus is the Alpha and the Omega. (Revelation 22:12-13)
- John the Baptist was to prepare the way for Jehovah. (Isaiah 40:3) John the Baptist prepared the way for Jesus. (Mark 1:1-4)
- Jehovah is the great Judge who renders to each man according to his deeds. (Jeremiah 17:10) Jesus is the only judge who renders to each man according to his deeds. (Revelation 2:23)
- Jehovah is the great shepherd who leads His people to water. (Psalm 23:1-2) Jesus is the shepherd who leads His people to water. (Revelation 7:17)
- Jehovah is Lord of Lords. (Deuteronomy 10:17) Jesus is Lord of Lords. (Revelation 17:14)
- The Father is Lord of all. (Matthew 11:25) Jesus is Lord of all. (Acts 10:36)

- Jehovah is the Savior. (Isaiah 45:21) Jesus is the Savior. (2 Peter 1:1)

This is just a sample of all the passages in the Bible that testify to Jesus' deity. Sadly, instead of just reading this information for what it plainly says, the Watchtower has indoctrinated Jehovah's Witnesses to come up with biased excuses for each passage. In making such excuses, Jehovah's Witnesses find themselves in the same heretical category as the Muslims, Mormons, and Progressive "Christians." No one in these groups believes they belong to a heretical cult, but their biased Bible interpretations prove otherwise.

All of this causes me to ask, why would I want to follow an organization like this? Why would *you* want to follow an organization like this? Why not adhere to what the Bible plainly teaches? God emptied Himself of His deity, He took on the role of a servant, and He laid down His life so that we can be forgiven and live with Him forever. That is the Good News of the Gospel of Jesus Christ!

OTHER BOOKS BY
THE AUTHOR

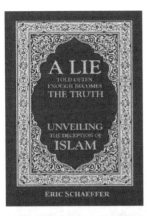

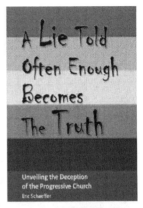

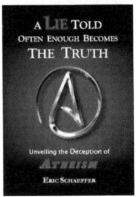

Printed in Great Britain
by Amazon